La Esperança

エスペランサ

1

かわい千草

Chigusa Kawai

La Esperança

Translation	Sachiko Sato
Lettering	Studio Cutie
Graphic Design	Eric Rosenberger
Editing	Stephanie Donnelly
Editor in Chief	Fred Lui
Publisher	Hikaru Sasahara

English Edition Published by
DIGITAL MANGA PUBLISHING
A division of DIGITAL MANGA, Inc.
1487 W 178th Street, Suite 300
Gardena, CA 90248

www.dmpbooks.com

First Edition: October 2005
ISBN: 1-56970-933-5

1 3 5 7 9 10 8 6 4 2

Printed in Canada

(La Esperança) エスペランサ

IF I AM EVER TO HURT ANOTHER

LET MY EXISTENCE BE ERASED

EVEN IF I SHOULD BE THE ONE TO SUFFER HURT

AS LONG AS IT MEANS THE HAPPINESS OF ANOTHER

SO THAT I MAY CONTINUE TO LIKE MYSELF.

La Esherança
エスペランサ

KREE
OH, GEORGES.
PRAYING THIS MORNING AS USUAL?
GOOD MORNING, SISTER.
GOOD MORNING.
IT'S A VERY GOOD THING.
I SEE THE COLLECTION HAS INCREASED AGAIN.
YES.
THAT CHALICE IN PARTICULAR IS THE PRINCIPAL'S FAVORITE.
I GATHER IT'S VERY EXPENSIVE.
NEVER LET ANY-ONE TOUCH!
FANATICAL GLASS COLLECTOR
IT'S BEAUTIFUL.
CRYSTAL?
ISN'T IT?
IT'S NOT FOR PRACTICAL USE, BUT
IT'S DELICATE AND VERY PRETTY.
I LIKE IT, TOO.
CLANG
CLANG
OH!
THAT'S THE FIRST BELL.
I'LL BE GOING.
SEE YOU AGAIN
YES.
SEE YOU.
CLANG

ギィ…
KREE
ROBERT!!
ZSHH
GAH
はっ
HUH?!
?!
WHAT ?!
SWOOSH

WHA?
IDIOT!
MOVE!
HUH?
WHOA!
WOBBLE
!
G--
ZSHH
WHIP

THUD

AN UN-KNOWN FACE...
はっ
RELEASE
WHOA!
ドサッ
WHUMP
?
TCH, IT'S A DUDE!
↑ HA HA
DON'T STEP OUT SO SUDDEN-LY!
I THOUGHT I WAS GONNA LAND ON YOU...
DAMN!
S...
SORRY...
BUT WAS IT MY FAULT?
I CAN'T BELIEVE IT.
YOU GET IT?
NEXT TIME, I'M NOT DODGING YOU!
WHAT ARE YOU DOING IN THE CHAPEL THIS EARLY IN THE MORNING, ANY-WAY?
ぽん…
PAT PAT
ザッ
ZTT

THAT'S NOT...
!
PAF ぱん...
OH.
ROBERT!! WHERE ARE YOU?!
COME TO THE PRINCIPAL'S OFFICE!!
ACK!
WHAT A PEST.
DANG!
ばっ
WHOOSH
JU--
HE SEEMS OLDER...
IS HE AN UPPER-CLASSMAN?
I SHOULD HAVE SAID THANK YOU.
OH!
WHEN I CATCH YOU--!
JOG
JOG
JOG
カラーン
CLANG
カラーン
CLANG

GOOD MORNING, GEORGES!
GOOD MORNING.
SAFE!
MORNING.
MORNIN'.
THAT'S UN-USUAL... YOU *BARELY* MADE IT.
DID SOME-THING HAPPEN?
UMM...
SOMEONE CAME RAINING DOWN FROM THE SKY...
...AND THE SISTER WAS RUNNING.
WHAT'S THAT?
MORNING, GEORGES.
GOOD MORNING!
THAT GEORGES IS NICE!
HMM HMM
SO SMALL AND CUTE.
IT'S NOT RIGHT, YOU KNOW.
KIND TO EVERY-ONE. EQUAL TO EVERY-ONE.
AROUND HIM, THERE ARE NO QUARRELS.
HIS MERE PRESENCE MAKES YOU FEEL LIKE IT'S GOING TO BE JUST ANOTHER PEACE-FUL DAY.
YUP YUP.
HEY HEY HEY!
DID YOU HEAR?!
BAM

MURMUR
ABOUT WHAT?
A NEW STUDENT--A TRANSFER STUDENT!
IN OUR CLASS!
WOW, THAT'S UNUSUAL.
DID YOU SEE HIM?
MURMUR
YEAH, YEAH!
WHAT'S HE LIKE?
MURMUR
HE'S BIG.
TALLER THAN ME OR ERWIN.
WHAT?
IS THAT ALL, GENIUS?
WHOOPS!
KCHAK
CLATTER
ALL RIGHT, NOW.
EVERYONE BE SEATED.
THE BELL HAS ALREADY RUNG.
CLATTER
CLATTER
OOHHHH...
OH...
IT'S HIM!
HMPH.
WHOA...
IGNORING ME?

WHAT'S SISTER DOING HERE?
DUNNO...
MAYBE HE'S SPECIAL.
THIS IS ROBERT JADE.
I HOPE YOU WILL ALL BE FRIENDLY TO HIM.
LET'S SEE. YOU CAN SIT NEXT TO RENAUD.
RENAUD, PLEASE HELP HIM BECOME FAMILIAR WITH THE CLASS.
MURMUR
YES SISTER.
MURMUR
NICE TO MEET YOU.
?
SAME HERE.
TUG
CLATTER
SST
HUH?
!
OH MY!
ROBERT, WHAT EVER ARE YOU DOING?!
YOU MUST PUT ON YOUR TIE--
IT'S A REGULATION HERE!
SO SLOVENLY!!
OOH...
OOHHH
OH OH OH
MY UNIFORM DOESN'T FIT.
MY SHIRT'S TIGHT, TOO.
SEE?
INNOCENT

OH,
IS THAT SO?
THEN I GUESS IT CAN'T BE HELPED.
OH
OH
UH
MURMUR
THEN I'LL HAVE THEM REORDERED FOR YOU IMMEDIATELY.
YES, THAT'S WHAT I'LL DO.
MURMUR
MURMUR
I'VE NEVER MET...
...SOME-ONE LIKE HIM BE-FORE...
I'M A LITTLE TAKEN ABACK...
MURMUR
MURMUR
MURMUR
HA HA HA HA
I WAS SHOCKED!
HEE
HEE HEE
WHEN YOU TALKED LIKE THAT TO THE SISTER...
HILARIOUS!
YEAH, THE REGULATIONS ARE STRICT HERE-- YOU SHOULD REALLY TRY TO STICK TO THEM, BUT...
THAT *WAS* FUNNY!
SO WHICH SCHOOL DID YOU GO TO BEFORE?
YOU'RE NOT IN THE DORMS, ARE YOU? DO YOU COMMUTE?
WHERE DO YOU LIVE?
CHATTER
CHATTER
WE'VE NEVER HAD A TRANSFER STUDENT BEFORE.
YEAH.
I'VE GOT IT!
I'LL SHOW YOU AROUND THE SCHOOL.
THERE'RE SOME GOOD SPOTS.
CHATTER
CHAK
NO, THANKS.
I CAN FIND MY OWN WAY AROUND.
THUNK
OH.
WHAT'S UP WITH HIM?
HUSH.

WHAT WAS THAT ALL ABOUT?!
EXTRA! EXTRA!
HEY!
HEY!
BIG NEWS!
THAT ROBERT GUY?
WHAT NOW?
HE'S OLDER THAN WE ARE!
OHHH
HUH, NO WONDER.
REALLY?
OH, IT'S JUST AS I THOUGHT.
SISTER WAS TALKING ABOUT IT!
BUT THEN WAIT A MINUTE!
HUH?!
THEN-- WHAT? HE WAS HELD BACK?!
WHAT?
WAIT!
ガタ CLATTER
YOU GUYS ...!
NO WAY! I WONDER WHAT HE DID?
OOHHH
ザワ
INTERESTING...
ザワ CHATTER
HE LOOKS SMART, THOUGH.
MAYBE HE WAS ILL?
...WHEN HE'S SO BIG AND HEALTHY?
AN ACCIDENT, MAYBE?
FOLLOWED BY A SUSPEN-SION...
WOW!
ザワ CHATTER
YEAH YEAH, I CAN DEFINITELY SEE THAT. HE PROBABLY DID SOMETHING.
HE DOES HAVE AN ATTITUDE.
WHOOAA...
ザワ CHATTER
THIS KIND OF TALK...
ズキ PANG
...IT PAINS ME.
ザワ CHATTER
ザワ CHATTER
ザワ CHATTER
WHOAA

カラ
CLANG
ROBERT!
THANKS FOR THIS MORNING.
MAY I CALL YOU BY YOUR FIRST NAME?
THAT'S THE NORM HERE.
UM...
SO, HOW DO YOU LIKE OUR SCHOOL?
IS YOUR HAND OK?
HOW DO I LIKE IT?
IT'S NOTHING SPECIAL.
WHAT DO YOU MEAN?
I'M GEORGES.
GEORGES SAPHIR.
AH...
UMM...
IF THERE'S ANYTHING YOU DON'T UNDER-STAND...
FEEL FREE TO ASK ME, OKAY?
......

WHAT?
FORCING YOUR KINDNESS ON ME?
OR...
...MAYBE IT'S JUST HYPOCRISY?
YOU FEELING SORRY FOR ME?
TH-
カァ
BLUSH
THAT'S NOT HOW I MEANT IT!
I'M SORRY.
HE'S RIGHT. GUESS I AM FORCING FRIENDLINESS ON HIM.
ばっ
WHIP
ザッ
TAP
OH.
THAT WASN'T MY INTENTION AT ALL, BUT...

CLANG
HE DIDN'T SHOW UP TO MASS *AGAIN* TODAY?
IT SEEMS THAT WAY.
THE SISTERS ARE MAD!
CLANG
BUT DON'T YOU THINK THEY'RE BEING TOO EASY ON HIM?
IF WE DITCH, WE GET CLEANING DUTIES AS PUNISHMENT...
MAYBE THE SCHOOL'S SCARED OF HIM, TOO?
I'M SURE HE DID SOME-THING BAD.
CLANG
AGAIN...
ROBERT!
YOU AGAIN.
WHAT NOW?
ACTUALLY, I JUST HAPPENED TO SPOT YOU.
WE HAVE MASS THREE TIMES A WEEK HERE.
YOU HEARD, RIGHT?
YOU SHOULD REALLY TRY TO FOLLOW THE SCHOOL REGULATIONS.
LIKE THE DRESS CODE...
THIS PLACE HAS TOO MANY RULES.
THE PRINCIPAL MUST BE HARDHEADED, LIKE A ROCK!
ROB-ERT...
SIGH
WHO CARES WHAT THE UNIFORM LOOKS LIKE AS LONG AS YOU'RE WEARING ONE?
BESIDES, DO I LOOK LIKE THE RIBBON-WEARING TYPE?
AND THE RELIGION THING IS *WAY* OVER-DONE.
PRAYER? *HA!* IT'S ALL A BIG *JOKE.*
MMPH
YOU *SHOULDN'T* THINK LIKE THAT.

UMMM...
WHAT, ARE YOU A TEACHER HERE?
DON'T ORDER ME AROUND.
I'M NOT ORDERING...
!!
OH!
WHA?
I GET IT! YOU'RE THE TEACHER'S PET!
NOW I SEE...
BLUSH
ROBER--
HAH
OH!
OH...
BA-THUMP
HUH?
DASH
WHAT'S WRONG WITH ME?
IT'S JUST A TRIVIAL MATTER.
THUMP
I HAVE TO BE MORE ACCEPTING...
THUMP
THUMP
... ...

GEORGES!
THE LIBRARIAN SAID THE BOOK YOU ASKED FOR CAME IN.
YOU CAN GO GET IT AFTER CLASS.
REALLY?
TA TA
THANKS!
HEY.
てへーん
JUMP!
ARE YOU THE ONE THAT'S BEEN SPREADING A LOT OF STUFF AROUND?
HE HE HE HE
EH?
EEEK
I'M SCARED!
I'M SORRRRRYYYY!
UM, UM, YOU SEE, IT'S LIKE THIS...
WELL...
I GUESS IT DOESN'T MATTER.
TELL ME ABOUT BLONDIE OVER THERE.
HUH?
THIS
BLONDIE?
YOU MEAN GEORGES?
!
COULD IT BE...
...THAT YOU FANCY HIM?
うおうっ
WHOA!
WHUMP
NEVER-MIND.
YOU FRIENDS WITH HIM?
IS WHAT I'M ASKING.
THIS IS WHAT I HATE ABOUT AN ALL-BOYS' SCHOOL...
HIERARCHY ESTABLISHED!

FRIENDS? WELL, YEAH.
HE'S FRIENDS WITH EVERY-BODY. HE'S WELL-LIKED BY EVERY-ONE, TOO.
HE DOESN'T SEEM TO HAVE ANY SPECIAL FRIEND-SHIPS, BUT...
HE'S *SERIOUSLY* DEVOUT.
THE TEACHERS LIKE HIM, TOO--BUT HE DOESN'T LET THAT GO TO HIS HEAD AT ALL.
OH...
I'VE NEVER SEEN HIM GET ANGRY.
I'D SAY HE'S GENTLE.
BUT THAT MAKES HIM SOUND LIKE THE PERFECT HUMAN BEING!
NO WAY...
OH YEAH! THAT'S IT! THAT'S WHAT HE IS!
BUT FOR ME HE'S MORE LIKE AN ANGEL.
YOU CAN'T BE SERIOUS.
RIDICU-LOUS!
DO YOU GUYS *REALLY* BELIEVE THAT?
THERE'S NO SUCH PERSON.
KCHAK
OH!
!!

OH NO!
JEAN'S BEEN CORNERED.
TCH
OOHHH
WHAT ?!
MURMUR
WHOA!
ROBERT...
NOT GOOD.
HUH?
WHO ?!
KCHAK
MURMUR
MURMUR
MURMUR
WH...
WHAT ARE YOU DOING WITH JEAN ?!
UH...
WHY ARE YOU MESSING WITH HIM?!
ACTU- ALLY...
RRGH!
YOU!
SHH
WHAT IT LOOKS LIKE.
SHUT UP!
WHAT ?!
JEAN...

THAT'S NOT HOW IT WAS, RIGHT?
OH...
GEOR...
HA!
HA HA!
I'LL BE DARNED.
HEH HEH
HEH

HOW HEROIC OF YOU.
WHAT A NICE GUY.
YOU'D EVEN SPEAK UP FOR ME, HUH?
INTERESTING...

MURMUR
YOU'RE THE ONLY ONE LIKE THAT.
SFFT
REALLY.
!
TUG

I AM GOING...
I HATE...
...PEOPLE LIKE YOU.
...TO RIP OFF YOUR MASK.
WHIP
はっ
HUH?
はっ
G--
WHAT'S WRONG?
WHAT DID HE SAY?
UH...

NO.

IT WAS NOTHING.

WHY?

CLANG

I WANT TO BE FRIENDS WITH HIM.

LIKE I AM WITH HENRI, AND JEAN AND EVERYONE ELSE.

BUT...

...HE'S GOT HIS OWN WORLD.

I CAN'T FORCE MYSELF INTO IT JUST TO GET CLOSE TO HIM.

BECAUSE THAT WOULD MAKE ME JUST LIKE THAT MAN.

HURTING SO MANY PEOPLE.

UNSCRUPULOUSLY CRUSHING THEIR SPIRITS.

I WOULD BECOME JUST LIKE HIM...

I SHOULDN'T GET CLOSE.

I SHOULDN'T HOPE FOR THAT.

OR ELSE...

...I'LL NO LONGER BE ABLE
TO LIKE MYSELF.
!
CLATTER
ガタ
EARNEST, AREN'T YOU?
HEH
WHAT ARE YOU SO JUMPY ABOUT? WERE YOU THINKING ABOUT ME OR SOME-THING?
HEH

...
...
I HEARD YOU CAN USUALLY BE FOUND HERE.
HOW PIOUS.
I'VE ALSO HEARD YOUR REPUTATION.
"AN ELITE STUDENT, BELOVED OF EVERY-ONE."
"SERIOUS AND KIND."
"LIKE AN ANGEL." ALL THAT.
CREAK
WHY ARE YOU SUCH A SWEET LITTLE BOY? FOR WHAT REASON?
I'M NOT THAT GOOD A PERSON.
NO REASON.
I JUST HAVE TO BE THIS WAY.
I CAN'T REALLY EXPLAIN, BUT,
IT'S MY IDEAL TO LIVE ACCORDING TO GOD'S TEACHINGS.
...SELF-MARTYR-DOM.

SACRIFICING YOURSELF AND LIVING FOR OTHERS? THAT KIND OF THING?
CHUCKLE
HOW *HYPO-CRITICAL*.
NO! IT'S NOT LIKE THAT!
THEN WHAT?
HAS ANY GOOD EVER COME OUT OF DENYING YOURSELF? HAVE YOU EVER *GAINED* ANYTHING?
GAIN?
AGAIN...
THEN WHAT ABOUT YOU? CAN YOU LIVE WITH YOURSELF FOR SELFISHLY DOING *WHATEVER* YOU WANT?
DO YOU LIKE YOUR-SELF?!

HA!
SURE! I LOVE BEING ME!
"WOW, LOOK AT ME! I DO ANYTHING I WANT! I'M GREAT!"
THAT'S WHAT I THINK!
CLATTER
AT THE VERY LEAST, I'M LIVING A HAPPIER LIFE THAN YOU.
JOLT
HAPPIER?
CREAK
HMPH.
WELL, WE'LL SEE JUST HOW LONG YOU CAN KEEP IT UP.
SLAM
......

......
LOVE MY-SELF...
HMPH! THAT'S A GOOD ONE.
CLANG カラーン
CLANG カラーン
REALLY! YOU'RE A SAVIOR!
I'M SUPPOSED TO BE HEADING OVER TO THE ORPHANAGE AFTER THIS, AND--
OH? IS SOME-THING WRONG?
OH? THE ORPHAN-AGE? WHAT'S IT LIKE?
HAH! は。
YES, WELL...
MOST OF THE CHILDREN LOST THEIR PARENTS IN AN ACCIDENT.
BUT THERE ARE SOME FROM FAMILIES SO POOR THAT THEY WERE NOT ABLE TO PAY BACK THEIR DEBT.
AND SOME LOST THEIR PARENTS TO SUICIDE.
TAKING ADVANTAGE OF THE POVERTY-STRICKEN...
LENDING THEM MONEY AT AN INCREDIBLE RATE OF INTEREST...
ALL FOR ONE'S OWN GAIN?
COME TO THINK OF IT, YOU LOST YOUR FATHER AT AN EARLY AGE TOO, DIDN'T YOU?
YES...

SIX YEARS AGO.
MY FATHER
WAS THAT VERY CULPRIT...
SISTER, YOU HAVE A TELEPHONE CALL.
OH.
THEN I'LL TAKE THOSE.
WOULD YOU?
UMPH.
WOBBLE
OOPS!
WH- WH- WH-
STUMBLE
WHOA!
CLATTER
THUD
CLATTER
YOU SURE HAVE BAD BALANCE.
DO YOU HAVE YOUR FEET ON THE GROUND?
RO--
WHAT!
THUMP
YOU'RE REALLY A GOOD LITTLE BOY, AREN'T YOU?
BEING FORCED TO CARRY ALL THESE...
FUMP

IT'S NOT LIKE THAT.

WHAT'S WRONG? GONNA GET ANGRY LIKE YOU DID YESTERDAY!

!

GO ON, GO ON.

OH!

BUMP

SORRY ABOUT YESTERDAY IT WAS WRONG OF ME TO CALL YOU SELFISH, WASN'T IT?

YOU'VE GOT YOUR OWN WAY OF DOING THINGS.

I CAN'T BELIEVE YOU. WHY DO YOU APOLOGIZE?

IT'S NO FUN.

WATCH OUT!

NEVER MIND THAT. WHY DO YOU CONCERN YOURSELF WITH ME?

I SEE.

BUT I DON'T THINK IT WILL EVER HAPPEN, THOUGH.

HEH HEH

I WONDER.

......

WHY ARE WE TALKING ABOUT THIS?

HE'S MAKING WAVES...
I HATE TO ADMIT IT.
BUT I THINK HE'S GETTING TO ME.
WHAT AN ODD SIGHT!
ROBERT LOOKS LIKE HE'S HAVING FUN!
I WONDER IF BEING TOGETHER WITH GEORGES WILL BE A GOOD INFLUENCE ON ROBERT?
WHAT ARE YOU THINKING?
...ABOUT WHAT YOUR DESIRES ARE.
I HAVE MALICIOUS INTENTIONS, JUST TO LET YOU KNOW.
HOW I CAN GET YOU TO THINK LESS ABOUT OTHERS AND MORE ABOUT YOURSELF.
WHAT DO YOU HOPE TO ACCOMPLISH BY CONCERNING YOURSELF WITH ME?
I...

I DON'T CARE ABOUT MYSELF AS LONG AS EVERY-ONE ELSE IS HAPPY.
NO ONE SHOULD BECOME UNHAPPY BECAUSE OF MY SELFISH EGO AND DESIRES.
WHY?
HE'S FOR-REAL?
COULD IT BE?
WHY GO TO SUCH LENGTHS TO STAY SO PURE?
THIS...
...IS THE ONLY WAY I KNOW HOW TO LIVE.
STUBBORN...
THEN...
...YOU'LL BE THE SORRY ONE.
?!
YOU WON'T BE ABLE TO LIVE THAT WAY FOR MUCH LONGER.
SISTER!

CAN YOU COME HERE FOR A MINUTE?
SLAM
BUT I'M IN THE MIDDLE OF SOMETHING.
JUST COME WITH ME!
WHAT IS IT?
TAP
FOR EXAMPLE-- SAY, HENRI IS A COFFEE MUG.
JEAN IS, LET'S SAY, A SOUP PLATTER ONE USES FOR DINNER.
TAP
THE SISTER-- THE CHALICE USED FOR MASS.
TAP
CREAK
IF I WERE TO COMPARE PEOPLE TO UTENSILS...
...YOU MOST RESEMBLE...
...THIS CHALICE.
OH!
PUT THAT BACK!
THAT'S THE PRINCIPAL'S MOST PRECIOUS BELONGING...
SMART BOY.
SQK

TAP
FOR WHAT REASON DOES IT EXIST?
...THIS THING.
"HOLY"
"PURE"
PROTECTED IN A GLASS CASE.
SPLISH
BA-THUMP
STOP!
"MUST NOT BE DEFILED"
"MUST NOT BE TOUCHED"
SPLASH
"NOT EVEN ALLOWED TO RECEIVE WATER"
"A DECORATION"

LOOK AT IT.

BEAUTI-FUL!

IT'S BEAUTIFUL.

DELICATE.

AND INFINITELY...

...FRAGILE!

はっ HAH!

WAIT!

STO--

SMASH
BAM
WHAT WAS THAT SOUND ?!
OH!
THIS...
GEORGES? WAS IT YOU?!
NO, IT WAS ROBERT !!
WE SAW THE WHOLE THING!
OH, MY!!
THE SHAT-TERED CHAL-ICE!
CLINK
OW!

WHY?
AAAAAAHH!!
WHAT HAVE YOU DONE ?!
OH!
KRASH
NOT YOU TOO!
IT'S ALL MY FAULT!
ROLL
BECAUSE OF ITS VERY BEAUTY.
BECAUSE OF ITS VERY DELICACY.
IT IS FRAGILE AND...
WEAK.
LIKE ME.
I'M GLAD IT WASN'T A SERIOUS WOUND.
I'M SORRY...

CHAK
SISTER, WE SHOULD BE GOING.
YES.
I KNOW... WHY DON'T YOU ACCOMPANY US?
IT'S THE ORPHANAGE I WAS TELLING YOU ABOUT EARLIER.
OH!
YES! I'D LIKE TO GO!
THUD
ARE YOU OK?
YEAH.
THANK YOU!

SIS-TER.
GEORGES...
THIS IS THE YOUNG TEACHER.
NICE TO MEET YOU.
!
YES.
HELLO.
THAT WAS THE CHILD.
THE ONE WHOSE PARENTS COMMITTED SUICIDE.
UM...
IS SHE FROM THIS TOWN?
NO, SHE USED TO LIVE IN VARMA.
I KNEW IT.
IT'S THE TOWN I USED TO LIVE IN.
SELFISH GAIN, SELFISH DESIRES.
ONLY BAD THINGS RESULT FROM THEM.
THEY ONLY BRING MISFORTUNE, LIKE WHAT THAT MAN DID...

...TO CHIL-DREN LIKE HER.
UMM, YOU KNOW WHAT?
MARIE WANTS TO BE LIKE THE YOUNG TEACHER.
MARIE WANTS TO GIVE STUFF AND DO STUFF FOR OTHER LITTLE KIDS.
ANYTHING THEY WANT!
I SEE.

WHAT DO YOU WANT, BIG BROTHER?
HUH?

UMM...
MAYBE I'M HAPPY WITH THE WAY THINGS ARE ALREADY?
WHAAAT?
YOU DON'T HAVE ANY-THING THAT YOU WANT?
NOTHING? NO WAY! MARIE HAS TONS AND TONS OF THINGS SHE WANTS!
UH, GUESS NOT.

THEN,
WHAT DO YOU WANT TO BE?
ME?
I'VE NEVER...

...THOUGHT ABOUT IT BEFORE.
WHAAAAT?
YOU DON'T KNOW THAT, EITHER?!

SORRY.
HEE HEE
HURRY UP.
HEE HEE HEE
WHY DO YOU APOLO-GIZE? YOU'RE FUNNY!
PAF
ぱん

MARIE LIKES YOU, BIG BROTHER!
LIKE?
ME?
YEAH.
'CUZ YOU'RE *NICE!*
MARIE'S GLAD SHE MET YOU, BIG BROTHER!
LIKES...
...*ME?*
MY FATHER IS THE ONE WHO RUINED YOUR LIFE.
YOU'RE A KIND GIRL,
MARIE...
I'M HIS SON.
IF SHE KNEW THE TRUTH...
...SHE'D PROBABLY...
MARIE, IT'S TIME FOR TEA!
YOUNG TEACHER!

REMEMBER TO WASH YOUR HANDS!
OKAAAY!
WHY DO YOU MAKE SUCH A FACE?

I'M...
I'M NOT WORTHY OF RECEIVING SUCH KIND WORDS.

......

I CAME HERE SEVEN YEARS AGO, TOO.

DUE TO AN *ENORMOUS* DEBT,

MY FAMILY WAS RUINED.

I'M FROM VARMA, TOO.

OH!
SHH...
GEORGES!
THE SITUATION BETWEEN OUR PARENTS DIDN'T MATTER.
WE USED TO PLAY TOGETHER A LOT.
I RECOGNIZED YOU IMMEDIATELY.
I *CAN'T* FORGIVE WHAT YOUR FATHER DID,
BUT I'VE ALWAYS LIKED YOU.
I'M SORRY...
YOU'RE STILL SAYING THE SAME THING.
I'M SORRY...
I'M SO SORRY!
THAT'S WHAT YOU WERE SAYING AS I WAS FLEEING THAT TOWN.
MARIE SAW YOU AND LIKED YOU.
SHE SAW YOU FOR WHO YOU REALLY ARE.

YOU'RE YOU, RIGHT?
I...
...LIKE YOU, TOO.
I'M...
ME...
I'M NOT MY FATHER.
ALL THIS TIME...

OH, COME NOW!
YOU'RE A MAN, AREN'T YOU?
YOU WERE STRONGER IN THE PAST!
NOW, NOW.
PAT ポン
PAT ポン
STAY HAPPY WITH YOURSELF,
OR YOU'LL BE THE SORRY ONE.
OH...
"YOU'LL BE THE SORRY ONE..."
THAT'S RIGHT.
CLANG カラーン
CLANG カラーン
WHY IS IT...
...I'VE WANTED SOMEONE TO TELL ME THAT.

...HE SAID THE SAME THING TO ME?

SHFFT
!

YOU...

YOU SAID I WON'T BE ABLE TO LIVE THIS WAY MUCH LONGER.
NOW I THINK I UNDER-STAND WHAT YOU MEANT BY THAT.
I THOUGHT DESIRING ANYTHING FOR MYSELF WOULD ONLY RESULT IN CAUSING SOMEBODY ELSE PAIN.
...THE SAME IF I ENTERED THEIR LIFE.

THAT'S WHY...
I DECIDED THAT I WOULD WANT NOTHING.
THAT I WOULD THROW AWAY ALL DESIRES.
WHY AM I SAYING ALL OF THIS?
BUT...
...THAT'S NOT HOW IT IS, IS IT?
IT'S ALL RIGHT FOR ME,
TO LIVE FOR MYSELF...
ISN'T IT...
HOPE...
I'LL ONLY SAY THIS...

FREE YOUR-SELF.
ROBERT !!

I...
I'M REALLY GLAD I MET YOU!
...
YOU'RE A STRANGE ONE.
カラーン CLANG

HOW GOES IT?
HAVE YOU GOTTEN USED TO THE SCHOOL?
THUNK
パタン
SO-SO...
...SIR.
IT'S ONLY BEEN TWO YEARS SINCE THE INCIDENT.
THOUGH IT WAS AN ACCIDENT, YOU LOST SOMEONE PRECIOUS TO YOU.
I KNOW YOU BLAME YOURSELF. YOU WERE SO GUILT-RIDDEN OVER IT THAT I HESITATED WHETHER TO BRING YOU TO THIS PLACE.
YOU MEAN, "IT'S ALREADY BEEN TWO YEARS."
I'M OVER IT.
FOR NOW,
I'M ENJOYING MYSELF THE BEST I CAN.
I SEE.
YOU CERTAINLY ARE.
I CAN'T GO ON LIVING
IF I CAN'T LIKE MYSELF.
THAT CHALICE WAS EXPENSIVE!
IT WAS A GENUINE VENETIAN!
AND FOLLOW REGULATIONS, TOO!
NO!
GRRR
STRESS CONTRIBUTES TO BALDNESS, YOU KNOW...

CLANG
カラ
WILL I BE ABLE...
TO FREE MYSELF?
CLANG
カラ
MY WORLD WILL CHANGE.
SOMETHING WILL CHANGE.
BUT...

...MAYBE I JUST HAVEN'T YET REALIZED...

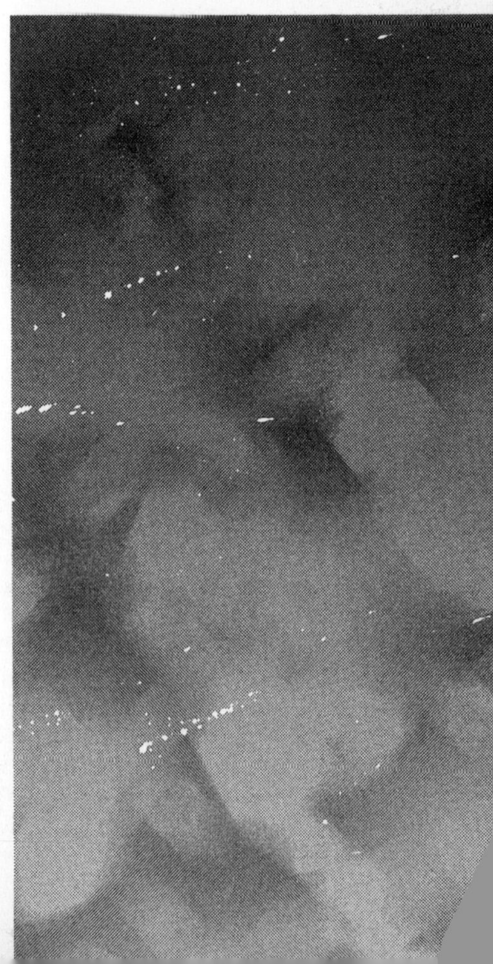

...THAT THERE'S MORE TO THE STORY...

La Esperança◆END

(Cathedral カテドラル)
AS YOU CAN SEE, THE CATHEDRAL IS ADJACENT.
IT IS QUITE ANCIENT, SO PORTIONS OF IT ARE PRONE TO CRUMBLING, AND...
SEVERAL SECTIONS OF THE BELFRY ARE EVEN OFF-LIMITS, SO I HEAR.
IF I REMEMBER CORRECTLY, YOUR ANCESTORS FINANCED THE CONSTRUCTION OF THIS CATHEDRAL.
BEYOND THE WALLS--TOURIST TOWN?
YES, BUT...
THE SCHOOL GROUNDS ARE VERY SPACIOUS.
THERE SHOULD BE NOTHING TO INTERFERE WITH YOUR STUDIES.
カラーン CLANG
カラーン CLANG
I SEE.

カテドラル
CATHEDRAL

YOU'RE NOT HANGING OUT WITH HIM LATELY, I SEE.
HUH?
ROBERT.
WASN'T HE DOGGING YOU FOR AWHILE?
IT WASN'T LIKE THAT.
I THOUGHT WE'D BE-COME...
...A BIT CLOSER, BUT...
SHFFT
OH.

GOOD MORNING, ROBERT.
YEAH...
THE ONLY THING THAT'S CHANGED...
GEORGES!
OH!
SORRY.
...IS THAT HE NOW RETURNS MY GREETINGS.
OH...
MR. SAPHIR!
COME WITH ME.
TAP
TAP
CHAK
PRINCIPAL.
I'VE BROUGHT HIM.
OH, THANK YOU VERY MUCH.
...

ARE YOU, GEORGES SAPHIR?
YES.
I SEE.
I'M SORRY TO CALL YOU IN HERE SO SUDDENLY.
I'VE HEARD A LOT ABOUT YOU FROM YOUR TEACHERS AND THE SISTERS.
I HEAR YOU'RE AN EXCELLENT STUDENT.
NOT AT ALL.
ARE YOU FAMILIAR WITH THE SOVEREIGN OF THIS COUNTRY?
YES.
YOU SEE, THE GRAND DUCHY OF ESPERANTO'S SOVEREIGN, THE GRAND DUKE ARGENT, HAS A SON.
WHO WILL BE ATTENDING SCHOOL HERE AT SAINT GROLLO.
ALL THE EDUCATION HIS SON, SIR FREDERIC, HAS RECEIVED UP UNTIL NOW HAS BEEN FROM HOME TUTORS.
IN OTHER WORDS, THIS WILL BE HIS FIRST TIME ATTENDING A SCHOOL.
DUKE ARGENT AND I ARE OLD FRIENDS.
AND THAT'S WHERE YOU COME IN.

AN OFFICIAL FRIEND?!
YES.
I THINK YOU'D BE PERFECT.
DON'T YOU THINK, SISTER?
...
BUT...
I DON'T THINK I COULD...
OH NO! THERE COULDN'T BE ANYBODY MORE PERFECT!
BUT...
THE GRAND DUKE ARGENT HIMSELF HAS REQUESTED *THIS* OF ME.
PLEASE, I ASK YOU TO ACCEPT.
YES.
OH NO, WHAT SHOULD I DO?
SLAM
WHAT A PERFECT CHOICE!
HE'LL DO JUST FINE!
YES, YES, TO A "T"!
YES.
IS SOMETHING THE MATTER?
OH...
IT'S NOTHING.

IT'S JUST THAT HE GREATLY RESEMBLES SOMEONE I KNEW.
HUH ?!
MURMUR ザワ
MURMUR ザワ
MURMUR ザワ
WHAT THE HECK IS AN "OFFICIAL FRIEND"?
HOW GRANDIOSE!
IS THAT ANY WAY TO MAKE FRIENDS?
WHAAAT ?!
COOL! A CLASSMATE?
THE LITTLE PRINCE ?!
HE RAND UKE'S SON ?!
IF YOU DON'T REALLY CARE ABOUT MAKING ANY TRUE FRIENDS? THEN YEAH, WHY NOT?
MURMUR ザワ
MURMUR ザワ
RRTT キィ
IT'S DUKE ARGENT!
IT'S THE REAL-DEAL!
WOW ワッ

AH, LONG TIME, NO SEE. SORRY TO IMPOSE ON YOU LIKE THIS.
NOT AT ALL.
チャ
KCHAK
WOW!
WHAT BEAU-TI-FUL
SIL-VER HAIR...
SIR FREDERIC...
HE IS TO BE YOUR OFFICIAL FRIEND.
OFFI-CIAL FRIEND?
FEEL FREE TO ASK HIM ABOUT ANYTHING YOU DON'T UNDER-STAND.
I'M GEORGES SAPHIR.
I LEAVE HIM IN YOUR HANDS.
OH!

WHAT BEAUTIFUL GOLD HAIR YOU HAVE!
UH NO, IT'S NOT ANY-THING SPECIAL.
IT'S COMMON-PLACE.
BLUSH
CHUCKLE
NO, NO!
THIS HAIR OF MINE HAS RECEDED SO BADLY.
BWA HA HA
RIGHT, PRINCIPAL?
MINE, TOO.
WA HA HA HA HA HA
HOW DO YOU DO, I'M GEORGES SAPHIR.
FLIT
NICE TO MEET YOU.
SHFFT
WHA?!
THUMP
SIR FREDE-RIC!
WAIT A MO-MENT.
IT'S UP TO YOU, MR. SAPHIR.
OH.
YES.
TA TA
"SILVER"... HOW UNUSUAL.

"EVERYONE ELSE IN HIS FAMILY HAS PLATINUM BLONDE HAIR."
"IT USED TO BE THAT THE FAMILY OF ARGENTS ALL POSSESSED LOCKS OF SILVER."
"IT IS A SIGN OF YOUR PROUD ANCESTRY."
"IT IS A SIGN THAT YOU'RE 'SPECIAL'."
"SIR FREDERIC."
"SIR FREDERIC."
SPECIAL
WAIT FOR ME!
TAK TAK...
SHALL WE GO TO CLASS?
UH...
HOW SHALL I ADDRESS YOU?
......
JUST ADDRESS ME NORMALLY.
HMPH
OH...
THEN IS "FREDDY" OKAY?

WHEW!

...

HE'S GOT SILVER HAIR! SILVER!

MURMUR

COOL! I'VE NEVER SEEN THAT BEFORE!

IS IT FOR-REAL?

MURMUR

WHAT ARE WE SUPPOSED TO TALK ABOUT WITH THE SON OF A DUKE?

IT MAKES ME NERVOUS!

MURMUR

YOU BUNCH OF GOSSIPS...

WHO CARES? WE'LL ***NEVER*** GET ANOTHER CHANCE LIKE THIS!

MURMUR

CHATTER

MURMUR

CHATTER

CLANG カラーン…
CLANG カラーン…
HEY.
HOW DO YOU DO, SIR FREDERIC!
IS YOUR FATHER WELL?
MURMUR ざわ
CLATTER ガタ
MURMUR ざわ
MURMUR ざわ
MURMUR ざわ
WHAT ARE YOU, STUPID? WE JUST SAW HIM!
DON'T BE SO NERVOUS.
QUIET! IT'S JUST STANDARD PROTOCOL!
SHUT UP!
KCHAK ガチャ
THUNK パタン
ANY QUESTIONS YOU HAVE, FEEL FREE TO ASK GEORGES!
WHAT'S WRONG WITH EVERY-ONE?
MURMUR ざわ
MY MOTHER IS A GREAT FAN OF YOUR FATHER!
CHATTER ざわ
GRAB
?!
WHAT ARE YOU TALKING ABOUT... HE'S THE GRAND DUKE'S SON!
HE'S *ROYAL-TY!*
MURMUR ざわ
CHATTER ざわ
OH YEAH!
MY LITTLE BROTHER IS NAMED AFTER YOU!

BA-THUMP
UMM...
MAY I ASK YOU SOME-THING?
BA-THUMP
BA-THUMP
WHAT IS IT?
IS THIS YOUR REAL...
SMACK
OW!
DON'T TOUCH ME!!
HUSH
STOMP
HEY!
WAIT...
YOU IDIOT!
WHOA
NOT GOOD!
FREDDY!
MURMUR
I'M GOING TO THE PRINCIPAL'S TO HAVE HIM *EXPELLED!*
HE'S INSOLENT!
?!
WAAIT A *MINUTE!*
STOMP
STOMP
STOMP

I AGREE THAT WAS WRONG OF BART...
BUT IT *DOESN'T* WARRANT EXPULSION!
ARE YOU TELLING ME WHAT TO DO?!
NO-- I!
SHUT UP!!
I'M GOING TO HAVE YOU *REMOVED* AS MY "OFFICIAL FRIEND"!!
THAT'S NOT POSSIBLE.
WHAT?!
IT IS AT YOUR FATHER'S REQUEST.
I CANNOT DO SUCH A THING WITHOUT HIS FURTHER PERMISSION.
AND BESIDES...
...FRIENDS ARE NECESSARY.
ABSURD!
DO YOU HEAR ME?
I HAVE NO NEED FOR YOU!
I'M ONLY SUFFERING YOUR PRESENCE BECAUSE THE PRINCIPAL *FORCED* ME TO!
GOT IT?!

OKAY.
DAMN!
WHAT IS FATHER THINKING?
SOMEONE LIKE YOU, *OF ALL PEOPLE!*
RUSTLE
THUD
EEP
?!
OH.
WHO THE *HELL* ARE YOU ?!
SCREECH
PAFH
WH--
...
...

I WONDER IF HE MADE HIS CHOICE BASED ON LOOKS.
A MATCHING SET.
WHAT ?! WHAT DOES THAT MEAN ?!
CHUCKLE
HE'S EVEN SHORTER THAN YOU.
!
HEH HEH HEH
H--
IF IT WAS ME, I WOULD HAVE BEEN STEPPED ON.
HOW RUDE !!
WHAT WAS THAT ALL ABOUT ?!
GRRR
!
THWAP
HMPH
WHAT AN *INSOLENT* GUY!
HE'S IN OUR CLASS, TOO.

HMPH.
A PROBLEM CHILD, HUH?
BOTH YOU AND HIM...
WHAT...
I DON'T LIKE EITHER OF YOU.
WHY DON'T YOU FAWN OVER ME?
CLINK
SO, HOW WAS SCHOOL?
AREN'T YOU HAPPY TO HAVE FRIENDS OF THE SAME AGE?
I KNOW I WAS.
NOT REALLY.
SUCH BOTHER-SOME THINGS.
CLINK
THEY'RE USELESS.
WHAT DID YOU SAY?

I WAS FINE BEING TUTORED AT HOME!
I DON'T UNDERSTAND WHAT YOU'RE THINKING, *FATHER!*
I'M DONE!
KCHAK
FREDE-RIC!
I DON'T CARE!
SIR FREDERIC, YOUR TEA IS READY.
I DON'T WANT ANY!
I'VE BEEN IN THIS WORLD 14 YEARS.
I'VE NEVER LACKED FOR ANY-THING.
I'M "SPE-CIAL," AREN'T I?
CLANG
WHAT NEED DO I HAVE FOR FRIENDS?!
OH!
YOU DUM-MY!
HA HA HA
OUCH!
YEAH, AND THEN...

!
GEORGES!
WHOA!
YES?
JUMP
I WANT TO SEE THE WEST TOWER!
GUIDE ME!
GEEZ...
OH...
OKAY.
WAIT UP!
GEORGES!
GEORGES!
GEORGES!
HEY!
THEY'RE SUP-POSED TO BE "OFFICIAL FRIENDS."
RIGHT?
OOPS, HE TRIPPED.
THEY'RE MORE LIKE MASTER AND SLAVE.

SMASH
MY HAND SLIPPED.
CLEAN THAT UP.
!
FREDDY...
...YOU'RE MY "OFFICIAL FRIEND", AREN'T YOU?
IF YOU DON'T LIKE IT, GO TELL THE PRINCIPAL!
TELL HIM YOU WANT TO QUIT LOOKING AFTER ME!
TO BE PERFECTLY HONEST, *I DON'T LIKE YOU!*
YOUR ATTITUDE, THE WAY YOU TALK, EVERY-THING!

カチャ…
CLINK
HMPH!
カラーン…
CLANG
カラーン…
CLANG
CLASS HAS STARTED.
HUH?
OH!
カタッ
CLATTER
OH YEAH.
MUSIC CLASS.
!
WHAT ABOUT YOU?
DITCHING.
……
ガタ
CLATTER

RIGHT.
I'VE GOT TO GO.
CLAK
YOU'VE GOT YOUR HANDS FULL.
WHAT?
IT'S FUN TO WATCH.
……

IT'S DIFFICULT.
I DON'T KNOW WHAT HE WANTS ME TO DO.
HE SAID HE DOESN'T LIKE EVERY-THING ABOUT ME.
I DON'T KNOW WHAT TO DO.
OR HOW...

……
!
YOU DON'T WANT TO BE HATED?
ARE YOU THAT SCARED OF BEING DISLIKED BY SOME-ONE?
THAT'S NOT...
HAH

UH...
CLATTER
ガタ
I'M RIGHT, *AREN'T I.*
ギ
CREAK
YOU...
...WANT TO BE LIKED BY EVERY-ONE.
MRRRGH
カ
NO.
I'M RIGHT.

OTHER-WISE...
...YOU WOULDN'T MIND SO MUCH.
RIGHT?
......
GRIP
G...
IF YOU DON'T LIKE IT, TELL ME TO STOP.
GO ON.
STOP!
GAA
HUFF
HUFF

IF YOU DON'T LIKE IT, SAY SO.
HUFF
G...
YOU SAY YOU DON'T CARE ABOUT YOURSELF?
YOU'RE WRONG.
YOU LOVE YOURSELF SO DEARLY YOU CAN'T STAND IT.
THAT'S RIGHT.
YOU'RE AFRAID OF GETTING HURT.
YOU'RE SCARED OF BEING HATED.
JUST SAY WHAT YOU MEAN.
BUT YOU CAN'T EVEN UTTER A SIMPLE THING LIKE THAT.
SHFFT

STOP IT!!
WHAP
HUFF
WHY...
HUFF
THIS...
HUFF
JUST LOOKING AT YOU...
HUFF
...BUGS THE HELL OUT OF ME!!
BAM
WHAM!!

SHIT!
WHAM
WHAT THE HELL AM I DOING?
TCH!
I SHOULD JUST LET HIM BE!
WHAM
RRGH!
DAMMIT!
HUFF
I'M SCARED...
HUFF
I'M SCARED OF THOSE EYES.
THEY PIERCE RIGHT THROUGH MY SOUL.
OW!
REVEAL-ING THINGS EVEN I DON'T WANT TO SEE.
I...

I'M SCARED OF HIM?

YOU DON'T WANT TO BE HATED?

THAT'S RIGHT.

I'M HATED.

BY FREDDY.

"YOUR DAD'S A BAD MAN, ISN'T HE?"

"MOM SAYS I SHOULDN'T PLAY WITH YOU!"

I NEVER...

...HAD ANY FRIENDS.

I'M SCARED OF BEING HATED?

"I HATE YOU!"

I SHOULD BE USED TO THIS BY NOW.

I'M SCARED OF BEING HATED?

H...
HATE...?
カラーン CLANG
SEE YA!
カラーン CLANG
CHAK チャ
はぁ… HAH
CLAK ガタ…
FREDDY.
ポーン… PLING
ギ… CREAK
す… SSS

"THE SWAN"*
*NOTE: A PIECE FOR CELLO, FROM THE "CARNIVAL OF ANIMALS" BY CAMILLE SAINT-SA S.

SO AS NOT TO OVERPOWER...

...THE CELLO.

PLINK

CLUNK
OH!
I'M SORRY...
DID I INTERFERE?
CLATTER
NOT REALLY.
OH.
I'M GLAD.
UMM, DO YOU PLAY THE CELLO?
CREAK
...
...
IT'S A NICE SOUND. I LIKE THE WAY YOU PLAY.
I DIDN'T HATE IT.
YOUR PIANO...
HUH?

YOU CAN ENTER THE CATHEDRAL NEXT DOOR FROM HERE.
OF COURSE ONLY THE SISTERS ARE ALLOWED TO, THOUGH.
WHAT'S THAT?
THAT'S THE BELFRY. BUT IT'S SO OLD THAT IT'S OFF-LIMITS.
I SEE.
SOME-THING WRONG?
NO.
HEY, GEORGES! CAN YOU COME HERE A SECOND?
OH!
OKAY.
EXCUSE ME, FREDDY.
!
WHAT?

THUMPA
SIR FRED-ERIC!
THUMPA
LOOK...
THUMPA
SIR FRED-ERIC!
LOOK AT ME...
FREDDY!
BA-THUMP
LOOK ONLY AT ME!!
GEORGES!!
YOU'RE STILL IN THE MIDDLE OF YOUR EXPLANATION!!
COME HERE!
OH!
SORRY.
GEEZ...
I DON'T ENVY HIS JOB.
"I'VE BEEN SUMMONED BY A TEACHER-- CAN YOU WAIT HERE FOR A BIT?"
I'VE NEVER HAD ANYONE KEEP ME WAITING BEFORE.
YOU, TOO?
HONESTLY,
I JUST DON'T KNOW HOW I'M SUPPOSED TO ACT AROUND HIM.
TAP
TAP

YEAH YEAH

LITTLE RICH KIDS ARE HARD TO HANDLE. THEY'RE NOT LIKE US COMMONERS.

I WONDER HOW GEORGES STANDS IT. IT MUST BE HARD ON HIM.

NO KIDDING.

TALK ABOUT *FINICKY*... I NEVER THOUGHT HE'D BE SUCH A *SPOILED* BRAT.

I'D HAVE QUIT GEORGES' JOB LONG AGO.

YOU'D NEVER BE CHOSEN IN THE FIRST PLACE.

HA HA HA HA

GAH! OH!

SLAM

TREMBLE SHIVER TREMBLE

YOU WERE STILL HERE?

SIR FRED-ERIC?!

STOMP STOMP STOMP

WAAAHHH

OH?

FREDDY? WHERE ARE YOU GOING?

TAT

HUH?

AT LEAST YOU'LL FOLLOW ME, RIGHT?

YOU WILL FOLLOW AFTER ME... WON'T YOU?

FREDDY!

WHIP

FREDDY!
ガシャーン
CLANG
...
...
ガシャン...
CLANG
ガシャン
CLANK
THAT'S RIGHT, FOLLOW ME.
カツーン
TAP
カツン
TAP
カツン
TAP
カツーン
TAP
FOLLOW ME!!
ザア...!
WHOOSH
HUFF
FREDDY...
HUFF

SEE...
WHY ARE YOU DOING THIS?
BA-THUMP
"I WONDER HOW HE STANDS IT."
... ...
IF YOU DON'T LIKE IT, THEN SAY IT.
LOOK AT ME.
JOLT
IF YOU HATE ME...
THEN JUST SAY IT!!
SEE ME FOR WHO I REALLY AM!!
FREDDY!
DASH

DON'T, FREDDY!
COME BACK OVER HERE!
DON'T YOU GIVE ME ORDERS!
I'M NOT ORDERING YOU! I'M *ASKING* YOU!
SHUT UP!
IT'S THAT HAIR OF YOURS I CAN'T STAND, EITHER!
?!
BOTH MY FATHER AND BIG SISTER... THEY'RE PLATINUM BLONDE! I'M THE ONLY ONE THAT'S DIFFERENT!
EVERYONE SAYS I'M *"SPECIAL"*!
THAT'S RIGHT-- I'M THE GRAND DUKE'S SON!
I'M *DIFFERENT* FROM EVERYONE ELSE!
BUT WHAT DOES "SPECIAL" *MEAN?!*
I NEVER ASKED TO BE BORN WITH *THIS* HAIR!
BUT... I LIKE YOUR HAIR.
IT GLITTERS IN THE SUN, AND IT'S BEAUTIFUL.
SHUT UP!
YOU'RE JUST LIKE ALL THE OTHERS... YOU ONLY SEE ME AS A CURIOSITY!
THAT'S NOT TRUE!

THAT COLOR BELONGS TO YOU. YOU ALONE!
IT'S NOT THAT IT'S "SPECIAL."
IT'S UNIQUE. YOURS AND NO ONE ELSE'S!
IT'S PROOF THAT YOU ARE YOU!
SHUT UP!
CRUMBLE
FREDDY!!
CLATTER
WHAP
G...

YOU HATE ME... DON'T YOU?
"I DON'T UNDERSTAND HOW..."
BE QUIET!
EVERYONE SAYS I'M DIFFICULT TO HANDLE.
...THAT THEY DON'T KNOW HOW TO INTERACT WITH ME.
"I CAN'T UNDERSTAND HOW..."
BE QUIET!
...THAT I'M JUST A SPOILED LITTLE RICH BOY.
...AND THEY CAN'T COPE WITH ME.
YOU'RE JUST THE SAME!
"I DON'T KNOW HOW TO INTERACT WITH HIM."
I KNOW THAT YOU WANT TO LET GO OF THIS HAND!
I KNOW YOU HATE ME.
I'M THE ONE THAT DOESN'T KNOW HOW!!
I'M NOT LETTING GO!

HOW CAN I?!
WHETHER I HATE YOU OR LIKE YOU...
OF COURSE I CAN'T DECIDE!
I DON'T KNOW YOU WELL ENOUGH YET!
THAT'S RIGHT.
ALL I KNOW RIGHT NOW IS...
I WANT TO LIKE YOU!
I DON'T YET KNOW...
...THE REAL YOU.
THAT'S WHY I'M NOT LETTING GO OF THIS HAND!
MURMUR
A PER-SON?
MURMUR
HEY!
WHAT'S THAT?
MURMUR
IS THAT A PER-SON?!

OH!

WHAT ARE THEY DOING?!

SOME-ONE CALL RESCUE!

MURMUR

DON'T GET TOO CLOSE! IT'S GOING TO CRUMBLE!

MURMUR

IT'S DANGER-OUS!

I SHOULD JUST LET HIM BE.

BUCKLE

NO!

NOOOO!

I CAN'T HOLD HIM MUCH LON-GER...

GRIP

FREDDY!

CALM DOWN! LOOK AT ME!

I PROMISE I WON'T LET GO.
I WANT YOU TO TRY TO CLIMB BACK UP SLOWLY, ON YOUR OWN.
?!
IT'S OKAY. YOU CAN DO IT.
BUCKLE
BUT!
I CAN'T!
GRIP
……
FREDERIC!
FLINCH!
IT'S ALL RIGHT! YOU'RE LIGHTER THAN I AM.
SO TRUST ME.

HUFF
CLATTER
UH!
ドッ
THUD

ガラ
CRUMBLE

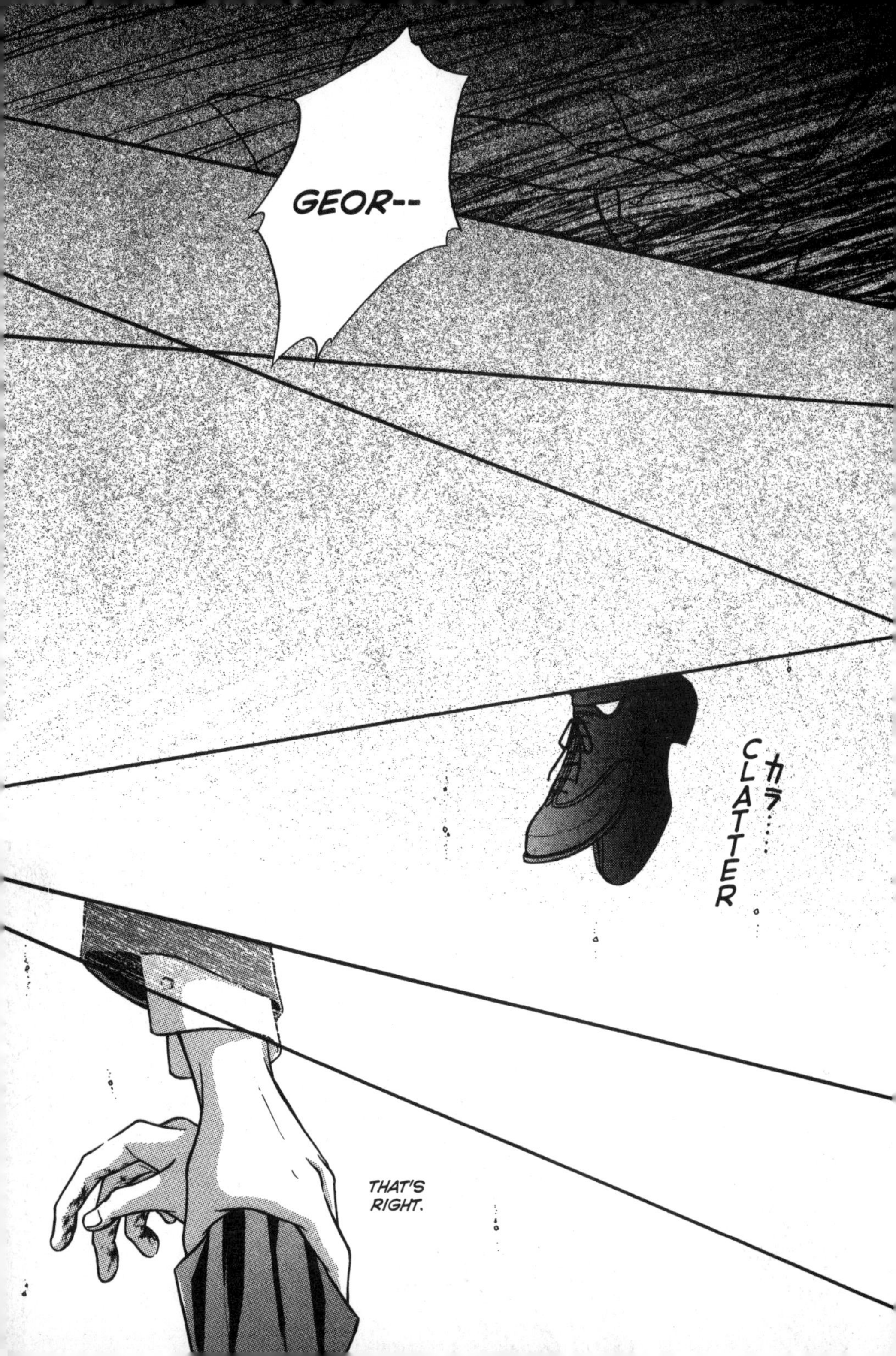
GEOR--
カラ……
CLATTER
THAT'S RIGHT.

YOU FOOL...
WHAT DO YOU THINK YOU'RE DOING?
I DON'T YET KNOW...
...THE REAL YOU.
ざわ MURMUR
ざわ MURMUR
ざわ MURMUR

THANK YOU.
STUPID...
CLAK
SLAP
ぱちん
OOHH!
ざわ...
YOU WENT TOO FAR.
......
I SEE YOU UNDER-STAND.
GOOD.
DOES HE MEAN ME?
ONE IDIOT SON IS ENOUGH.
WA HA HA!

OK, OK.
SORRY FOR THE COMMOTION, EVERYONE.
MY APOLOGIES.
NOTHING TO SEE HERE!
PRINCIPAL!
IT'S ALL RIGHT.
I WILL MAKE PROPER APOLOGIES TO THE BISHOP LATER.
ざわ.. MURMUR

NOW, THEN...
BOTH OF YOU--YOU ARE TO BE CONFINED TO YOUR HOMES FOR THREE DAYS' SUSPENSION.
WHAT? BOTH OF US?
IN A FIGHT, BOTH PARTIES ARE EQUALLY GUILTY.
CAUSING SUCH A RUCKUS IN THE CATHEDRAL.
DON'T WORRY. I'LL TAKE RESPONSIBILITY, TOO.

AND STAY QUIETLY AT HOME TOMORROW!
ISN'T THAT JUST TAKING A DAY OFF?

YOUR SHOULDER...
YOU SHOULD HAVE IT LOOKED AT.
SINCE YOU PLAY... THE PIANO.

CLANG
CLANG
OKAY...
BAD LUCK, HUH?
BEING GROUNDED LIKE THAT.
MMM.
BUT I DID GET TO GO TO THE HOSPITAL.
THERE WAS NOTHING THE MATTER.
I WONDER IF HE'LL COME IN TODAY-- THE LITTLE PRINCE.
AFTER THAT FUSS HE CAUSED.
CHAK
MAYBE HE CAN'T.
THE DUKE WAS HERE TO APOLOGIZE.
CREAK
HUSH
BLUSH
OH!
HEY, YOU.
CLAK

I BET YOU'LL GO BALD LATER IN LIFE.
えっ
WHAT?
R... ROBERT?!
THEY SAY PEOPLE WHO PART THEIR HAIR LIKE YOURS ARE SUSCEP-TIBLE.
MEANIE.
ゲッ
ACK!
ゲッ
えっ
かあっ
BLUSH
YOU!

どっかん
BABOOM
WHAT ABOUT YOU, THEN?!
AND ANY-WAY...
NO MATTER HOW YOU LOOK AT IT, YOU'RE THE ONE THAT'S OLD!!
うっ...
GSH...
PFFT!
ピ
TWITCH
WAS THAT YOU JUST NOW?
THE...
NOW, NOW!
THE WAY YOU PART YOUR HAIR HAS NOTHING TO DO WITH IT.
PROBABLY...
YEAH!
I'VE HEARD IT'S HERED-ITARY.
OK?
RIGHT?
POP
HEREDITARY.
UPPE CLAS MAN LOWE CLAS MAN RELA TION SHIP.
AAAAHH
NNNNOO
NO IT WAS-N'T!
ぎゃはははは
BWA HA HA HA HA
HE HASN'T GOT A CHANCE!
DOOOM
HUH?
WHAT?
OH!
SORR-
HERED-ITARY... HERED-ITARY.

WA HA HA
MY DAD'S SHOWING SIGNS, TOO.
IT'S OK.
YOU'RE STILL YOUNG.
RIGHT?
HA HA HA
CHATTER
OF COURSE I AM!
HOW RUDE!
YOU CALLED HIM "OLD"... NICE ONE!
CHATTER
HA HA
CHATTER
BUT BALDNESS IS CAUSED BY MALE HORMONES, ISN'T IT?
WHAAT?
DOES AGE HAVE ANYTHING TO DO WITH IT?
CHATTER
BUT...
THERE ARE COOL WAYS TO GO BALD, YOU KNOW.
CHATTER
LIKE HOW?
STOP SAYING "BALD"!
あっはっはっ
HA HA HA
DID YOU DO THAT ON-PURPOSE?
MAYBE.
OH, YEAH.
ABOUT THE COOL WAYS TO GO BALD...
STOP TALKING ABOUT BALDNESS!!
Cathedral END

(Ro・Ta—運命の輪—)
Ring of Fate
IF YOU DON'T LIKE SOME-THING, THEN SAY SO.
YOU'LL FEEL RELIEF WHEN YOU DO.
TO BE CLEARLY TOLD THAT YOU ARE HATED...
THAT WOULD BRING A KIND OF RELIEF, TOO.

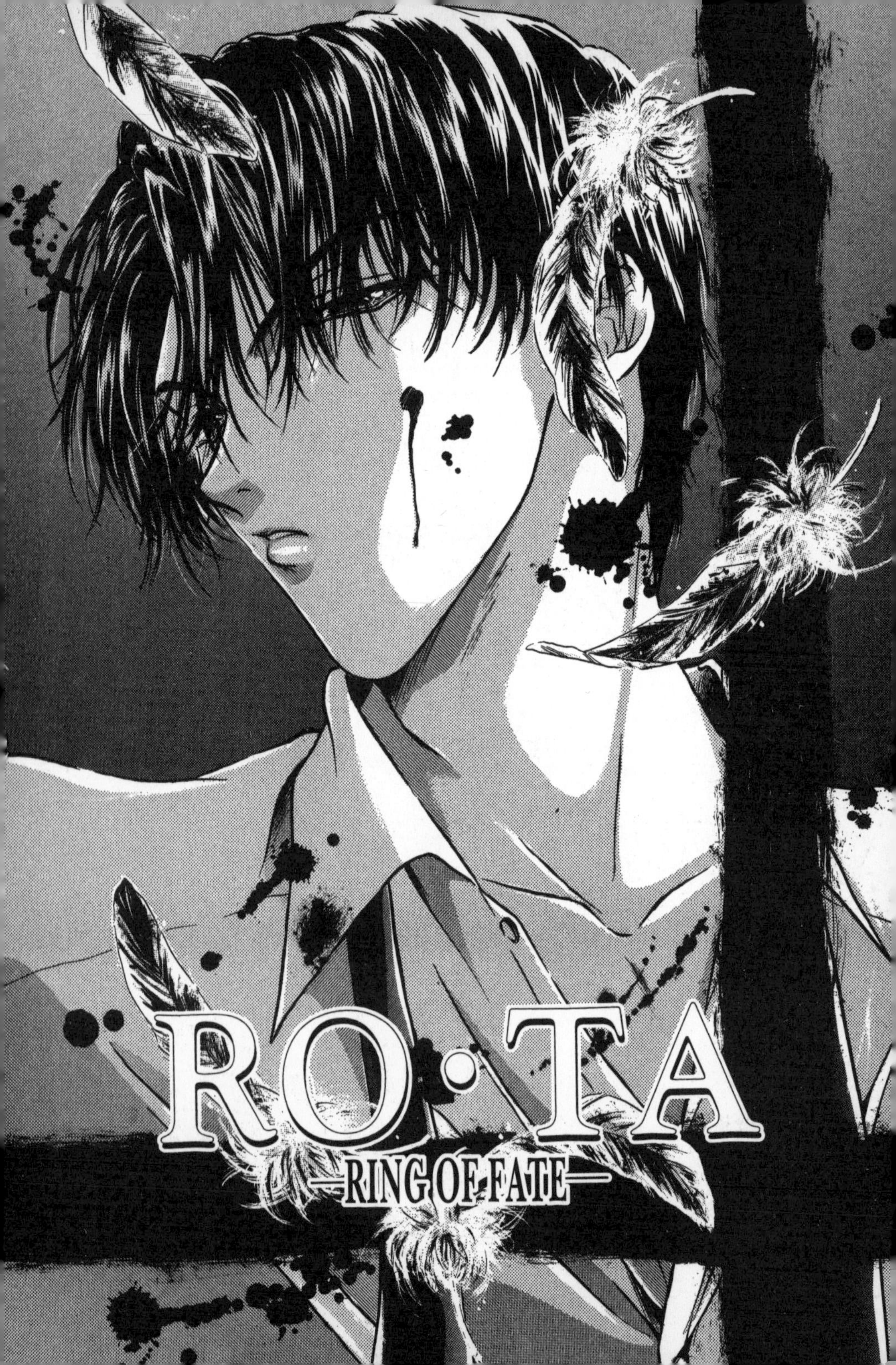
RO·TA
—RING OF FATE—

HI, GEORGES.
WERE YOU VISITING THE CHAPEL?
YEAH.
I HEARD THE PRINCIPAL'S COLLECTION HAS INCREASED AGAIN.
MORE CHALICES?
YEAH.
OH! THAT REMINDS ME!
THAT'S RIGHT! LISTEN... YESTERDAY...
WHAT?
SHFFT
WHOA! SERIOUSLY?
TAP
HI.
YOU...

...YOU'RE ABOUT TO BE ABDUCTED BY ROYALTY.
HUH?
ズ ZZT
HEY, YOU!!

I'M YOUR OFFICIAL FRIEND!
SNAP
STOP ACTING FRIENDLIER WITH SOMEONE ELSE!
ESPECIALLY HIM!

SIR FREDDY, COME HERE!
HERE'S HOW WE COMMONERS AMUSE OURSELVES.
BOOK
STOP CALLING ME BY THAT HALF-CASUAL HALF-FORMAL NAME!
DON'T PUT "SIR" IN FRONT OF A NICK-NAME!

FREDDY!
YOU SHOULDN'T POINT!
......
SO, THIS IS YOUR PERSONALITY?
THERE'S JUST SOMETHING ABOUT THIS GUY I DON'T LIKE!!!

I'M GLAD HE'S FITTING IN EVEN BETTER THAN I *EVER* COULD.
THAT WAS QUICK!
AAGH! WHAT IS THIS?!
BWA HA HA HA HA HA
わはははは
HEY...

SO,
YOU'RE THE SAME TOWARDS EVERY-ONE?
!
NO MATTER WHAT KIND OF PERSON THEY ARE.
NO MATTER WHO IT IS.
WHY DO YOU SMILE AT THEM ALL EQUALLY?
BECAUSE I WANT TO TRUST PEOPLE.
THEN...
...WHY IS IT THAT YOU STILL DRAW A LINE OF DISTANCE?
JOLT
ISN'T THERE A CONTRA-DICTION?
A LIE IN YOUR ACTIONS?

TAP
カツ…
ROBERT!
CLANG
カラーン
UH, LET'S SEE...
IT'S HENRI, RIGHT? THE ONE THAT'S ALWAYS AT SPARKLY BLONDE-BOY'S FEET.
SPARKLY
WOW-- YOU REMEMBERED.
AND I'M TALLER THAN HE IS, YOU KNOW.
WELL, I'VE ALWAYS HAD A GOOD MEMORY.

WHY DO YOU CONCERN YOURSELF WITH HIM SO MUCH?
WHAT?
I'VE NEVER SEEN HIM WEAR AN EXPRESSION LIKE *THAT* BEFORE...
ONLY AFTER YOU ARRIVED.
WHAT'S YOUR INTENTION?
HEH
HMPH.
SORT OF LIKE THE PLEASURE OF DEFLOWERING A VIRGIN, PERHAPS?
THERE'S NOTHING MORE ENTERTAINING THAN DEFILING SOMETHING PURE.
DON'T YOU THINK?

...IF THAT'S YOUR ONLY REASON,

I WON'T JUST STAND IDLY BY.

I'M HIS FRIEND.

BUT...
...I WONDER IF YOU CAN CLEAR THAT HURDLE.
WHAT ?
GETTING CLOSE WHEN PUSHING AWAY...
JUST WHAT IS IT THAT YOU WANT TO DO?
CLANG
CLANG
CLANG
I HAVE JUST ONE THING TO SAY...

JUST SEE TO IT THAT YOU GRADUATE.

...
...

TWIRL
くるん
YOU SHOULD KNOW THAT MY GRADES AREN'T A PROBLEM.
OH, WHAT A NICE DAY.
THAT IS MY CHAIR!!
AND YOU ARE A STUDENT HERE!!
GET UP!

OH, DEAR.
WHAT ABOUT YOU, THEN? SHOULD YOU BE SUMMONING ME FOR SUCH PERSONAL REASONS?
SQUEAK
キュル
I AM THE PRINCIPAL!!!
I DEAL OUT PUNISHMENT TO TROUBLE-MAKERS!!
SKIP-PING MASS!
DITCH-ING CLASS!
BREAK-ING EQUIP-MENT!!
AM I NOT CORRECT?!
YES, YES YOU'RE ABSO-LUTELY COR-RECT.

PUT YOURSELF IN MY POSITION.
SIGH...
OK, OK.
I GET IT.
くす CHUCKLE
CHUCKLE くす
CHUCKLE くす
くす
I KNOW I'M JUST...
A TROUBLE-MAKER.
は HAH!
ROBERT...
I'LL BE ALL RIGHT.
FATHER.
DIDN'T I SAY?
......
バタン THUMP

WHY AM I AT SCHOOL?
NO MATTER WHERE I AM, IT'S THE SAME.
I HAVE NO REASON FOR LIVING.
I DON'T KNOW WHAT TO DO WITH MYSELF.
SHFFT
WHO IS THAT?
CREAK

WHAT A CLICHÉ OF A CHARACTER.
RUSTLE
WHY?
WHY ARE YOU HERE IN THIS SCHOOL?
I DON'T THINK...
...YOU SHOULD GET TOO CLOSE TO ROBERT.

HENRI!
HE'LL ONLY HURT YOU!
HENRI...
I'VE...
I'VE KNOWN YOU SINCE WE WERE FIRST AT SCHOOL TOGETHER, SO I THINK I CAN SAY I KNOW YOU PRETTY WELL.
YOU'RE ALWAYS REASONABLE AND YOU NEVER ERR--
BUT YOU'RE JUST *TOO* TRUSTING OF OTHERS!
IT'S NOT *IN* YOU TO DOUBT PEOPLE AT ALL!
I KNOW YOU CAN'T HELP THAT.
BECAUSE THAT'S THE WAY YOU ARE.
BUT NOT HIM.
YOU TWO ARE *TOO* DIFFERENT!
HE'S *NOT* LIKE YOU!

I...

WHAT? IS SOME-THING WRONG?

I WAS JUST THINKING THIS IS THE FIRST TIME WE'VE EVER TALKED ABOUT SOMETHING LIKE THIS.

!
THANKS, BUT I'LL BE OKAY.

——"WHY DO YOU DRAW A LINE OF DISTANCE FROM THEM?"——

GEORGES?
PINCH

——"ISN'T THERE A CONTRADICTION?"——

"A LIE IN YOUR ACTIONS?"

IT'S TIME FOR CLASS-- LET'S GO.

WHY IS IT...

...IT'S ALWAYS THE SAME.

HIS WORDS.

THEY PIERCE ME TO THE CORE.

RE-VEALING THINGS ABOUT ME,

I DON'T WANT TO SEE.

BUT HIS WORDS...

THEY ALWAYS MANAGE TO LEAD ME TO THE LIGHT.

PULSE...

YOU'RE WRONG, HENRI.
YOU'RE TOO TRUSTING!
IT'S BECAUSE I KNOW HOW TO DOUBT...
THAT I WANT TO BELIEVE...
NO MATTER WHO IT MAY BE.
STOMP
MADD, FROM THE BASKETBALL TEAM--HE'S AT IT AGAIN!
HE'S PICKING A FIGHT AGAIN UNDER THE GUISE OF A GAME!
YOU THERE! QUIET!
STOMP
HE PICKS A FIGHT WITH ANY-ONE!
WHO IS IT THIS TIME?
STOMP
STOMP
STOMP
IT'S THAT NEW GUY? WUTSIZ-NAME?
ROBERT JADE.
CLATTER

YOU'RE THE NEW GUY, RIGHT?

PRETTY TALL.

COME ON, MAN, CUT IT OUT.

I GUESS IT'S TRUE ABOUT YOU BEING OLDER.

LET'S HAVE A GAME.

YOU AND...

HEY!!

ARE YOU IGNORING ME?!

LISTEN TO ME!

AND SO BRISKLY, TOO!

TAP TAP TAP TAP

BAM

!

YOU DON'T HAVE TO RUN AWAY.

TUNK TUNK TUNK

IT'S NOT AS IF WE'RE PICKING A FIGHT WITH YOU.

LET'S HAVE A GAME.
SHFFT
ROBERT!
YOU'RE IN THE WAY.
TUG
FWOOSH
!

WELL, NOW! LOOK WHO'S HERE.
IT'S THE ANGEL WHO LIVES IN THE CHAPEL.
YOU'RE AS CUTE AS THEY SAY.
SSHH!
COULD IT BE THAT YOU TWO ARE FRIENDS? AN ELITE STUDENT LIKE YOU?
THE FLOWER OF OUR CAMPUS?
OR IS IT SOME-THING MORE?
THUMP
ポン
SLAP

TUNK
ターン…
IT'S ME YOU WANT TO TAKE ON...
...ISN'T IT?
HE'S FAST!
HMPH!
SHFFT
HE'S GOING TO SCORE FIRST-- *THREE POINTS!!*
BAM

BAM
SHUFFT
SWISH
......
THWAP
!
WHA--
THUNK
BAM
BAM
BAM
HUFF

THUMP
FFFT
SWOOOOSH
TUNK
TUNK
TNK
TNK

SATISFIED?

!
THAT TOOK NO TIME AT ALL.

ザ
RUSTLE

ス
SHSSH

HEY, MR. ELITE STUDENT.

WHAT'S THE RELATION-SHIP BETWEEN YOU TWO?
WE'RE CLASS-MATES.

SHFFT

HMM...

ROBERT!

YOUR TIE.

YOU FORGOT IT.

OH.

THANKS.

THAT WAS *GREAT!* I WAS *SURPRISED!*

AND IT ALL HAPPENED SO QUICKLY.

YEAH?

THEN AS A REWARD...

...WANNA GIVE ME A KISS OR SOME-THING?
?!
HUH?!
HMPH.
I'M JUST HARASSIN' YA.
DON'T TAKE IT SO SERIOUSLY, STUPID.

STUPID.
...
...
DO YOU TWO KNOW EACH OTHER?
...WHAT MAKES YOU THINK THAT?
OH!
JUST A FEELING.
AM I WRONG?
YOU...
...ARE PRETTY FAMOUS, AFTER ALL.
I DON'T LIKE IT.
OH.
"ANGEL."
"ELITE STU-DENT."
BEING CALLED THOSE THINGS.
OH.

BACK THERE...
FOR SAVING ME...
THANK YOU.
FOR WHAT?
YOU KNOW.
NEVER MIND ALL THAT.
JUST QUIT INVOLVING YOURSELF WITH ME ALREADY.
IT'S NOT THAT I'M INVOLVING MYSELF...
THEN DON'T HANG AROUND SO MUCH!
BUT...
STAY AWAY FROM ME!
OTHER-WISE...
...
WHAM
I MAY JUMP YOU.
FOR-REAL.

バッ
WHIP
HMPH.
YOU WOULDN'T.
YOU CAN'T.

PULSE
ヮ...
WHY?
WHAT WOULD YOU KNOW?
SHUFFLE
I THINK...
...THIS IS THE FIRST TIME FOR ME...
...FEEL-ING LIKE THIS.
OVER-COMING REJECTION TO STEP INTO SOMEONE ELSE'S WORLD.
"FREE...
...YOUR-SELF."
I WASN'T SUPPOSED TO BECOME INTERESTED IN SOME-BODY ELSE'S LIFE, BUT...

...HE NEVER LEAVES MY MIND.
ザリ...
CRUNCH
INDIRECT, AREN'T YOU.
IT'S BEEN A WHILE.
ON A CAMPUS THIS HUGE, NO WONDER I DIDN'T SEE YOU SOONER.

YOU SEEM MORE SPIRITED THAN I THOUGHT YOU'D BE.
WHEN DID YOU IMPROVE YOUR GAME LIKE THAT?
SIGH
MAYBE I SHOULD HAVE STAYED OUT OF SCHOOL FOR ANOTHER YEAR.
NO, DON'T WORRY. I'LL BE GRADUATING IN SIX MONTHS.
WE ALREADY SETTLED THE GAME.
BUT...
WHAT YOU REALLY WANT TO TALK ABOUT IS SOMETHING ELSE, RIGHT?
YOU'VE ALWAYS BEEN LIKE THAT.
YOU ALWAYS TAKE *EVERYTHING* AWAY.
I DON'T LIKE YOU.

CRUNCH
OH.
IT'S HIM. HOW ELEGANT.
HE'S GOT NOTHING TO DO WITH YOU.
ATTRACTED...
...TO THE *PURITY* AGAIN?
FWAP
!

WHUMP

......

ANYONE INVOLVED WITH *YOU* GETS ON MY *NERVES*.

AND IF THEY SHOULD LIKE YOU, ALL THE MORE REASON.

THERE'S NO ONE.

YOU'RE IMAGINING THINGS.

WHAP

HA!

WE'LL SEE ABOUT THAT!

GH...
IT'S YOUR FAULT.
JOLT!!
IT'S YOUR FAULT THAT SHE DIED!!
...
...
SHE MAY HAVE DIED IN AN ACCIDENT...
BUT YOU BETRAYED HER!
YOU BETRAYED MY TRUST!!
SMACK

KOFF KOFF
NO RESISTANCE?
HA!
TUG
UGGH
YOU THINK YOU CAN LIVE A CALM, PEACEFUL LIFE?
YOU HAVE NO RIGHT TO ANY HAPPINESS!!!

SMASH
HAH
WHAT WAS THAT?
THUD
HUFF
WHOOOSH
HMPH.
YOU KNOW YOU CAN USE YOUR FATHER'S AUTHOR-ITY.
YOU COULD EVEN HAVE ME EXPELLED...
BUT I BET YOU WON'T EVEN DO *THAT*.
I'M AWARE OF ALL THAT.
HUFF

THAT'S WHY I HATE YOU.

RATTLE

!

THAT GUY!

ROBERT!
BLOOD...
DRIP

THUD
R--
ROBERT!!

HIS HEAD WOUNDS ARE NOT THAT DEEP.
HE JUST HAS A SLIGHT CONCUSSION.
WHERE'S THE PRINCIPAL?
HE'S NOT IN. I'LL CONTACT HIM.
THUMP
GEORGES,
YOU WERE THE ONE WHO FOUND HIM, RIGHT?
JUST WHAT IN THE WORLD HAPPENED?
I...
I DON'T KNOW, EITHER.

OH MY--
ARE YOU HURT, TOO?!
AND YOUR JACKET?
OH...
IT'S NOTHING.
RUB
OH, NO.
YOU MUSTN'T WIPE ON YOUR SLEEVE!
...
BA-THUMP
NO...
YOU...
BA-THUMP
FAULT...
BA-THUMP
NO...
YOUR...
BA-THUMP
TO...
SO...
IT'S OUR...

IT'S YOUR FAULT!!

JOLT!

UH...

ROBERT.

BA-THUMP!

UHH!

!

HAH

AHH

—IT'S NOT HER—

SIGH.

WH...

I WAS WORRIED.

ARE YOU ALL RIGHT? WE'RE IN THE INFIRMARY.

GET OUT.

BUT...

I TOLD YOU... DON'T GET INVOLVED WITH ME.

I'M NOT INVOLVED.
IT'S JUST THOSE WOUNDS...
IT'S NOT ANY OF YOUR CONCERN!
BUT...
SHUT UP!
DON'T HANG AROUND ME ANY-MORE !!
IT GETS ON MY NERVES !!
BUT...
G...
I'M WORRIED ABOUT...
GRAB

THAT'S WHY...
I TOLD YOU...
BE DEFILED.

SLAM
UHH!
BUMP
!
CLICK
CLACK
CLICK
...
...

HEY!
GEORGES?

OH!
THERE YOU ARE.
I HEARD YOU WERE HURT? ARE YOU OK?

ガチャ KCHAK

GEORGES!

グッ THUMP

は HA

HUH?
UH...
WHAT?

YOU'RE ACTING A LITTLE FUNNY. ARE YOU OK?

OH...
UMM...

WHAT ?!
HE WALKED HOME ?!
YES. HE'S RESTING NOW. HE SAID HE HAD A HEADACHE.
OF COURSE HE DOES! HE HAS A *CONCUSSION!* I GET A SUDDEN PHONE CALL AND WHAT DOES IT TURN OUT TO BE ABOUT? *THIS!*

OH! BUT SIR...
I KNOW... I'M JUST GOING TO CHECK ON HIM.

コンコン
TAP TAP
チャ
CHAK
WHAT IS IT?
OH, YOU'RE AWAKE?
HOW'S YOUR HEAD?
IT SUCKS.
IT'S YOUR OWN FAULT FOR BEING SO RECKLESS.

CREAK
ギシ…
WHAT WERE YOU THINKING?
AND THE CAUSE?
……
WHO DID YOU FIGHT WITH?

WASN'T I TELLING YOU JUST THE OTHER DAY?
BUT NO! YOU JUST...
I SAID MY HEAD HURTS!

YOU'RE RIGHT.

ANYWAY, YOU'RE GROUNDED. THREE DAYS SUSPENSION.
GET YOURSELF TO THE HOSPITAL TOMORROW.

THUMP
HMPH.
THE REASON I SHOW UP TO SCHOOL AT ALL...

WHO DO YOU THINK I DO IT FOR IN THE FIRST PLACE?

CLANG カラーン…

LANG カラーン

PANG ズキッ

OW!

SERVED YOUR TIME?

WHAT DO YOU MEAN?
DON'T PLAY DUMB! HE'S BEEN IN A DAZE THESE TWO TO THREE DAYS!
AND EVEN WHEN I ASK, HE WON'T TELL ME ANYTHING!
OH, SHUT UP.
IF HE SAYS NOTHING, IT MUST BE NOTHING.
JUST LEAVE HIM ALONE.
WHAT ARE YOU, HIS MOTHER?
MRGH!
ALL RIGHT, FORGET IT!
BUT IF YOU MESS WITH HIM AGAIN, I WON'T STAND FOR IT!!
!
DON'T WORRY.
SHFFT
TAP
THERE WON'T BE ANY MORE OF THAT.

ガチャ
KCHAK
SHFFT
AH, OW...
HEH
くっ…
HEH HEH
くく…
OKAY.
THINGS WILL QUIET DOWN.

ざわ RUSTLE
ざわ RUSTLE
ざわ RUSTLE

I DON'T KNOW.

WHAT SHOULD I BELIEVE IN?

WHAT I FEEL...
THUMM
CLOSE MY EYES...
IN MY HEART...
NOW.
WHAT DO I SEE?
CLANG
THUMM
WAFT

OHHH, WELL IF IT ISN'T LITTLE MR. SAPHIR.
THIS IS A SHORTCUT, ISN'T IT?
FROM THE MUSIC ROOM...
FOOF
GAG KOFF
SHFFT
OH.
THAT'S RIGHT. ELITE STUDENTS *AREN'T* USED TO THIS STUFF.
YOUR FACE IS LOOKING PRETTY, AS USUAL.
HA HA!
WEREN'T YOU INJURED AT ALL?

HMM...
GRIND
ザリ…
WE GO WAY BACK, HIM AND ME.
MUST BE SOME KIND OF DESTINY.
I WOULD NEVER HAVE BE-LIEVED...
I SWEAR...
...THAT SOMEONE LIKE YOU EXISTED.
...I ALMOST DOUBT MY OWN EYES.

ROTA.

I DON'T REALLY CARE WHAT YOUR RELATIONSHIP IS.
BUT IF ANYONE TRIES TO GET INVOLVED WITH HIM...
...I WON'T STAND FOR IT.
WHAT DO YOU MEAN?

I'M SURE OF IT.
YOU'RE GOING TO GET HURT.
......

DO YOU MEAN...
...AT YOUR HANDS?
!
HENRI?
...
CRUNCH
ザッ

GEORGES?
WHO'S THAT WITH HIM...
HAH

!!

THAT FOOL!
RUSTLE
HUH!
ROBERT?!
THUD!!

はッ
WHIP
I DON'T KNOW ANYTHING ABOUT HIS PAST.
I DON'T KNOW WHAT YOU TWO HAVE BEEN THROUGH.
AND I DON'T KNOW WHAT IT IS THAT YOU SEE IN HIM.
YOU SAID YOU WOULDN'T INTERFERE WITH HIM ANYMORE!
G...
THIS IS A WARNING.
HE WILL HURT YOU.

HE MAY EVEN BREAK YOU.
!
TCH.
I DON'T CARE...
...ABOUT THAT RIGHT NOW!
SHOVE
HEY!
WAIT!
EVEN SO...
...I'LL TRUST IN HIM.

I'LL BELIEVE IN THE ROBERT,
THAT ONLY I CAN SEE.
I FEEL THAT IT'S OKAY TO TRUST HIM.
THAT'S RIGHT.
HUFF
IN ME.
PULSE
ハ
HA!

HOW VERY QUAINT...
AND DOES THAT INSIGHT, ARISE FROM YOUR *BEAUTIFUL* SENSE OF FAITH?
I DON'T KNOW.
THEN...
!
YANK
...I'LL JUST HAVE TO MAKE YOU LOSE THAT FAITH!
WHOOSH
SLAP

UHH...
WHIP
MRGH!
WHY... YOU...

?!

WHOOSH

GRIT
... ...
HMPH.
DO AS YOU PLEASE, THEN.
BUT I ***WON'T*** ALLOW IT.
SOONER OR LATER, YOU'LL COME TO REGRET IT.

IN THE END...

...AREN'T YOU JUST GOING TO REPEAT THE SAME FATE?

I BET YOU'RE THE ONE WHO CHOSE HIM.

WHIRL

HUH?

OH!

IS THAT YOU, GEORGES?

OH!
SISTER! I CAN HELP YOU!
HENRI...
IT'S ALL RIGHT.

DO YOU NEED SOME-THING CARRIED?
OH, HELLO HENRI.

UHH...
I'M SORRY 'BOUT LAST TIME...
CRUNCH
HUH?
IN THE INFIRM-ARY.
OH... THAT.

I'M NOT WORRIED ABOUT THAT.
IT WAS JUST LIKE A KIND OF... GREETING, RIGHT?
I KNEW THA--

......
RELIEF
かぁはっ
OH, GOD!
I'M SOOO GLAD!
I WAS AFRAID YOU MIGHT HAVE SOME KIND OF WEIRD MISUNDER-STANDING.
OH, MAN! WHAT WAS I THINKING? I'M SO UNCOOL!
WOW.
HAH.
WHIP
ばっ
SO YOU CAN MAKE AN EXPRES-SION LIKE THAT!
MAKE THAT FACE IN CLASS, TOO!
OK?
MRRGH.
SHUT UP! WHY SHOULD I?
THERE'S NOTHING TO GAIN BY IT.
DON'T LOOK AT ME.
WHY NOT?

OHHH.
THAT HENRI...
I DUNNO.
SIGH
HENRI WILL BE OK.
PROBABLY.
WHY DO YOU DRAW THE LINE WITH HIM, TOO?
BE-CAUSE I'M AFRAID,
OF PLAYING FAVORITES.

GET-
TING
CLOSE
TO
PEOPLE...
IT'S
EASY
TO BE
FRIEND-
LY WITH
THEM...
BUT...
BUT
SOME-
WHERE
INSIDE...
I
DON'T
KNOW
HOW.
I
DON'T
KNOW
HOW.
I
CAN'T
BECOME
CLOSE
WITH
THEM.
BE-
CAUSE
OF
THIS
BAR-
RIER...
...I
CRE-
ATED
UNCON-
SCIOUS-
LY.

...IT'S WHAT I DESIRE.
MAYBE WE'RE ALIKE.
OUR INNER SCARS...
THAT AWKWARD-NESS...
THAT'S WHY WE'RE DRAWN TO EACH OTHER.
SO YOU'RE NOT GOING TO ASK... ABOUT ME?

YOU CAN TELL ME...

THINGS UN-SEEN...

THINGS UN-KNOWN...

...WHEN YOU FEEL LIKE TALKING ABOUT IT.

THINGS...

I BELIEVE IN...

...
...

BUT FOR NOW...

...ISN'T IT ENOUGH TO JUST "HAVE FUN"?

THAT'S FUNNY COMING FROM YOU.

YOU THERE! WHY ARE YOU FLIRTING WITH EACH OTHER FOR?!
OH, GOD.
THAT KID!
HIS LINE OF REASONING IS MESSED UP...
HUH?!
GET AWAY FROM EACH OTHER!!
WHAT ARE YOU SAYING?
FREDDY?!
I TOLD YOU NOT TO BE FRIENDLY WITH ANYONE ELSE BUT ME!!
WHY YOU...!!
GRRR んが!っ
ばばん
BABOOM!
YOU'RE STANDING TOO CLOSE!
WHAT RUMORS HAVE YOU FED? EH?
BOOK
ぱ。
THWAP
HEY!
GIVE IT BACK!
WAAH!
DON'T ACT SO BIG! YOU'RE ONLY A REGULAR CLASSMATE OF HIS!!
DUMMY.

YOU DUMMY!
THAT'S NOT TRUE, SHORTY.
OH OH OH OH
WE'RE PALS.
HOW DO YOU LIKE THAT?
WHAAAAT?!
DON'T CALL A SHORT PERSON "SHORTY"!
HOW RUDE!
OH?
SO YOU ADMIT TO BEING SHORT?
ROBERT!
THE RING OF FATE--HAS IT BEGUN TO MOVE?

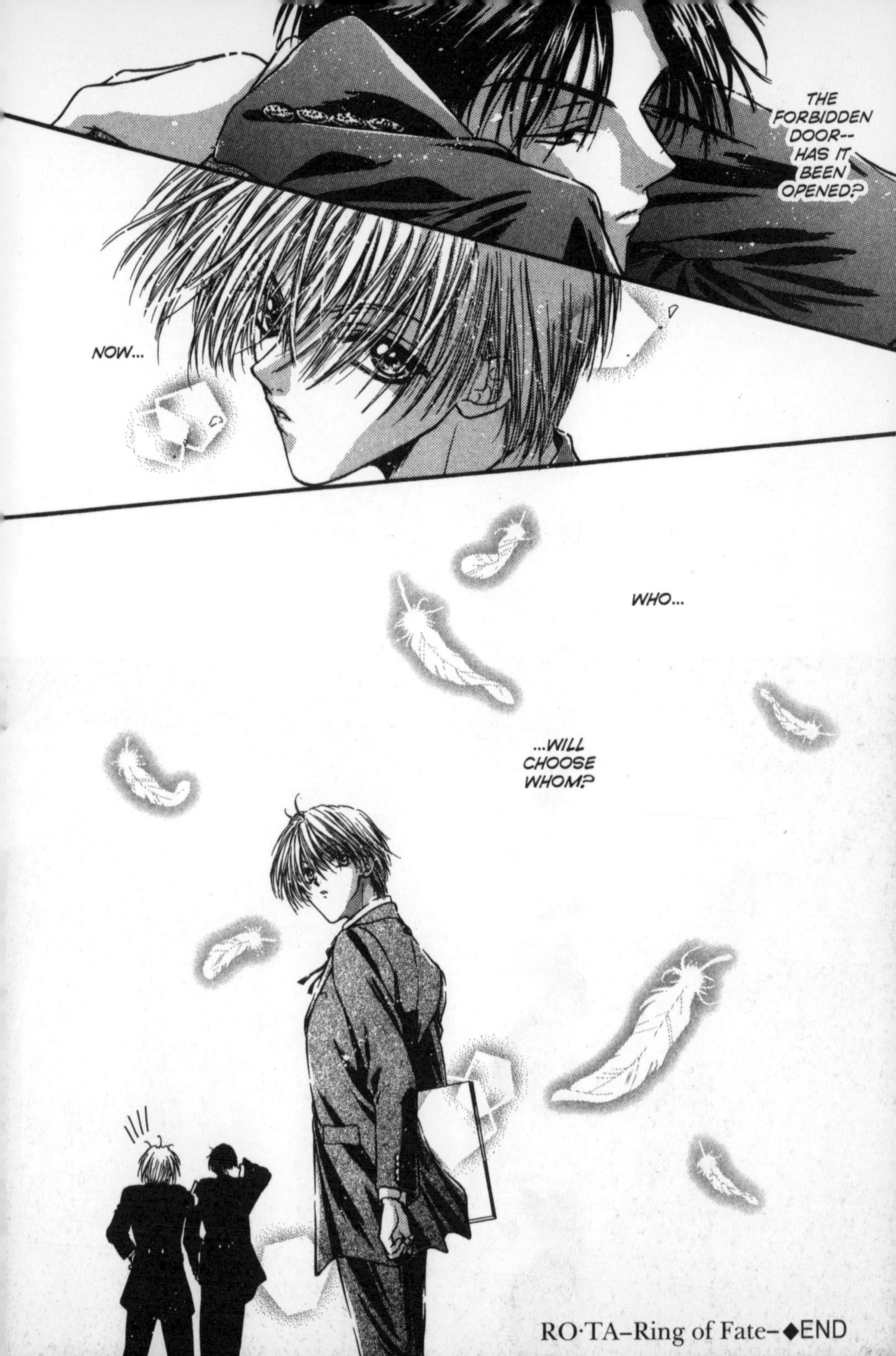
THE FORBIDDEN DOOR-- HAS IT BEEN OPENED?
NOW...
WHO...
...WILL CHOOSE WHOM?
RO·TA–Ring of Fate–◆END

Preview
THE KEY TO THE DOOR...
...WAS A SINGLE PHRASE.
I HATE...
...PEOPLE LIKE YOU.

SELFISHLY DOING *WHATEVER* YOU WANT.
CAN YOU LIVE WITH YOUR-SELF?!
SURE.
I LOVE MYSELF.
THIS IS THE ONLY WAY,
I KNOW HOW TO LIVE.
FREE YOUR-SELF.
I'M GLAD I MET YOU.

IF YOU HATE ME, THEN JUST SAY IT!
YOU'RE SCARED OF BEING HATED, AREN'T YOU?
YOU HYPOCRITE.
STOP!
YOU'RE WRONG!
JUST LOOKING AT YOU...
...BUGS THE HELL OUT OF ME!
BAM
DECIDING WHETHER I LIKE YOU OR HATE YOU...
I DON'T KNOW YOU WELL ENOUGH YET.
WHAT DO YOU THINK YOU'RE DOING?

HEY.
LET'S HAVE A GAME.
DON'T GET INVOLVED WITH ME.
I'LL JUMP YOU FOR REAL.
I WOULD NEVER HAVE BELIEVED THAT SOMEONE LIKE *HIM* EXISTED.
I DOUBT MY OWN EYES.
HE'S GOT NOTHING TO DO WITH YOU.
IT'S ME YOU WANT TO FACE.
ANYONE WHO HANGS AROUND YOU,
CAN'T REMAIN UNINVOLVED.
SMASH
I BET YOU'RE THE ONE WHO CHOSE HIM... WASN'T IT?!

YOU'LL BE HURT IF YOU REMAIN NEAR HIM.
I DON'T KNOW ABOUT HIS PAST, BUT...
I BELIEVE IN THE ROBERT ONLY I CAN SEE.
IT'LL TURN OUT THE SAME WAY.
I WON'T FORGIVE YOU.

HIS EXPRESSION...
IT'S MORE CASUAL LATELY.
I WONDER IF IT'S BECAUSE OF ROBERT...
MAYBE.
STOP IT...
DON'T!
HE WON'T DO ANYTHING FOR YOU...
YOU...
DON'T YOU LEAVE ME TOO...

BUT I'M RIGHT HERE...
DON'T CRY...
HE'S AN *EXACT* IMAGE.
YOU'RE JUST CONFUSING THE TWO OF THEM.
THIS IS ALMOST LIKE "LADIES FIRST"!
DO YOU *REALLY* THINK OF ME AS A BOY?
HE'S TOO SIMILAR.
IN EVERY WAY.
IN PURI-TY...
IN BEAU-TY...
HE'LL NEVER ALLOW YOU HAPPINESS.
IN DEVO-TION...
IT'S THE SAME ALL OVER AGAIN.
IT'S A PUNISH-MENT FROM GOD.
IN LOVE...
AND THAT IS WHY...

HE WAS BORN A MAN.
HAVE I GONE IN-SANE?
ANY-MORE....
DON'T HURT YOURSELF ANYMORE...
THOSE WORDS...
I SAY THE SAME TO YOU.
LEARN TO PUT YOURSELF BEFORE OTHERS.
ISN'T IT REALLY *YOU?*
WILL THIS MAKE YOU HAPPY?
WHO CHOSE *HIM?*

SMACK!
DO YOU EVEN KNOW...
...WHAT YOU'RE SAYING?!
ALL THE LIES...
I'M TIRED OF THEM...
JUST GIVE IN TO INSANITY...
IT'S OKAY FOR YOU TO THINK OF YOUR OWN GOOD, ISN'T IT?
SOME-ONE IS WITH ME...
I DON'T KNOW...
I DON'T WANT TO BE ALONE...
WHAT I SHOULD DO?
THAT'S UP TO YOU.

WHETHER IT'S RIGHT...
OR WRONG...
WHETHER TO GO ON...
OR QUIT.
ALL OF THAT...
EVEN IF IT MEANS COMMITTING A SIN...
IT'S YOUR CHOICE.

THIS HAND--
TO TAKE IT...
...OR NOT TO TAKE IT...

to be continued……

WHO'S THIS?
GEEZ

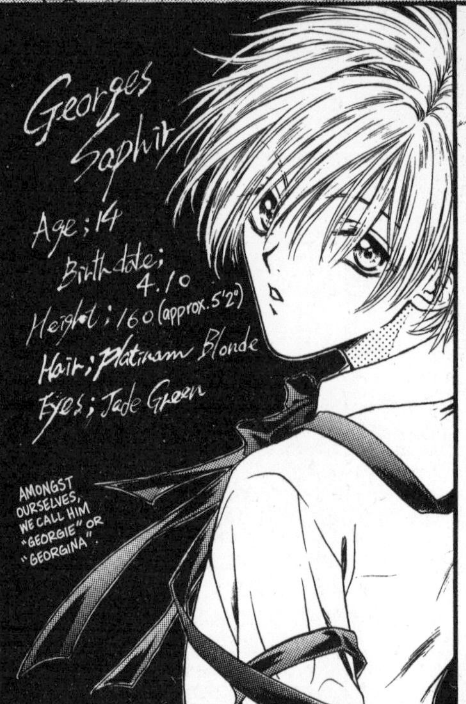

Georges Saphir
Age; 14
Birthdate; 4.10
Height; 160 (approx. 5'2")
Hair; Platinum Blonde
Eyes; Jade Green
AMONGST OURSELVES, WE CALL HIM "GEORGIE" OR "GEORGINA".

Promenade

ONE

IT'S FINALLY OUT! THE FIRST VOLUME! WHEEE! BOTH TO THOSE OF YOU WHO ARE NEW TO MY WORK AND TO THOSE WHO ARE NOT, HELLO. I'M CHIGUSA KAWAI. AS I AM WRITING THIS, THIS BOOK HAS, OF COURSE, NOT BEEN PUBLISHED YET - BUT HOW DID YOU LIKE IT? (WAS IT GOOD?) THERE ARE SO MANY THINGS I WANT TO SAY, BUT I DON'T KNOW WHERE TO START OH, I'LL JUST BEGIN WITH COMMENTARIES (EXCUSES?) FOR THE VARIOUS EPISODES (WHAT? YOU DON'T NEED IT? THEN LET'S SKIM OVER IT)

NOTE: THE CHARACTER DATA IS CURRENT TO THE TIME OF THE FIRST CHAPTER...IN THE MAGAZINE, GEORGES HAS ALREADY AGED A YEAR...

@ CHAPTER 1 - LA ESPERANCA (GEORGES' TALE)
→ I REMEMBER THE WEIGHT OF THE MANUSCRIPT BEING VERY HEAVY. IN THIS, THE THIRD WORK SINCE MY DEBUT, I GAVE IN TO THE SCREEN TONE DEMON IN ME (I REMAIN ONE TO THIS DAY...). FAMILIAR ALREADY TO THOSE IN THE KNOW, THIS STORY HAS A PAST HISTORY. I'M GLAD IT FINALLY GOT TO SEE THE LIGHT OF DAY. BY THE WAY, ESPERANCA MEANS HOPE IN PORTUGUESE. THE COMMON LANGUAGE SPOKEN IN THE STORY WORLD IS (SUPPOSED TO BE) ESPERANTO.

@ CHAPTER 2 - CATHEDRAL (FREDDY'S TALE)
→ THE CATHEDRAL ITSELF NEVER MAKES A PROPER APPEARANCE, DOES IT...BUT I KEPT IT AS THE TITLE BECAUSE IT MADE SUCH A NICE IMPACT. (HOW RANDOM) OH - AND WE'RE ALWAYS OPEN FOR CATHEDRAL GIRL APPLICANTS.

@ CHAPTER 3 - RO·TA -RING OF FATE- (ROBERT'S TALE)
→ RO·TA IS PRONOUNCED ROW-TA. THIS CHAPTER HAS A BIT OF A SETTLED-IN FEEL TO IT (KIND OF A "YOU GUYS MAKE A GOOD PAIR, SO ENOUGH ALREADY" FEEL). BUT IN ACTUALITY, THE STORY'S JUST BEGUN...PLEASE FOLLOW ALONG WITH ME ~

@ PREVIEW
→ 50% BLUFF, 30% LIES, 15% PROJECTED IMAGE MAKE UP THIS PREVIEW...(WHAT HAPPENED TO SERIOUSNESS?) (LAUGH) LET'S JUST SAY MY PLANS ARE UNDECIDED... HEH HEH HEH...

Robert Jade
Age; 17
Birthdate; 2.24
Height; 184 (approx 6')
Hair; Dark Brown
Eyes; Deep blue
AMONGST OURSELVES, WE CALL HIM "ROBE-ROBE".

Alain
Age; 18
Birthdate; 1.27
Height; 187 (approx 6'1")
Hair; Ash Brown
Eyes; Green
THIS CHARACTER'S NAME HASN'T BEEN MENTIONED YET.

I DON'T THINK IT WOULD BE GOOD TO COMMENT TOO MUCH ON THE STORY ITSELF BECAUSE I BELIEVE IN THE IMPORTANCE OF THE ORIGINAL IMPRESSION RETAINED AFTER READING THE STORY. IN MY OWN WAY, I PONDERED VARIOUS THINGS WHILE WRITING THIS STORY...SO IF THAT SENSE HAS BEEN SUCCESSFULLY CONVEYED, THEN I'LL BE HAPPY. (BUT I REGRET THAT I'M NOT MORE SKILLFUL, THAT I WOULDN'T BE PLAGUED WITH CORRECTIONS ON A DAILY BASIS, ETC.)

WELL NOW, THE NEXT TIME WE MEET WILL BE IN A NEW CENTURY. COOL! THIS VOLUME HAS SOME MEMORABLE INCIDENTS ATTACHED TO IT, LIKE THE TIME I WAS ON MY WAY TO DELIVER THE COLOR PORTION OF THIS MANUSCRIPT AND GOT PULLED OVER FOR SPEEDING. WHEN THE NEXT VOLUME COMES OUT, IT WILL CONTAIN AN EPISODE ABOUT ERWIN. PROBABLY. SO THOSE OF YOU WHO ARE FANS OF HIS, LOOK OUT FOR IT (ARE THERE SUCH PEOPLE)? THANK YOU FOR READING MY BOOK? SEE YOU NEXT TIME.

A CERTAIN DAY IN OCTOBER, 2000

Chigusa Kawai

Special Thanks

(THE PEOPLE I'VE TROUBLED TO GET THIS FAR)

to

R. Ochi
A. Marizune
M. Hori

◆

C. Kobayashi
J. Harada

◆

FokN 7

◆

Friends of mine
My Family
ALL MY RELATIVES.

◆

SHINSHOKAN
MR. K TANI

◆

and You

Henri Quartz
Age; 14
Birthdate; 7.11
Height; 167 (approx 5'6")
Hair; Black
Eyes; Aqua Blue

I TOOK HENRI'S NAME FROM THE "FATHER OF THE RED CROSS," JEAN HENRI DUNANT. ↑ KNOW HIM?

ISBN# 1-56970-928-9 $12.95

OUR KINGDOM
When the Prince falls for the Pauper...
The family inheritance will be the last of their concerns.
Written & Illustrated by
Naduki Koujima
DMP
DIGITAL MANGA PUBLISHING
yaoi-manga.com
The girls only sanctuary
ISBN# 1-56970-935-1 $12.95
Our Kingdom © 2000 Naduki Koujima

Café Kichijouji de
Welcome to the most unruly café in town...
...where, tempers rise, mop handles swing, giant boulders crash and repair bills soar.
So... kick back, pour yourself something hot and get ready to snack at
Café Kichijouji!
Café Kichijouji de 1
DMP DIGITAL MANGA PUBLISHING
ISBN# 1-56970-949-1 $12.95
ISBN# 1-56970-948-3 $12.95
ISBN# 1-56970-947-5 $12.95
www.dmpbooks.com
A New Wave of Manga
DMP
Cafe KICHIJOUJI DE © KYOKO NEGISHI/ YUKI MIYAMOTO 2001.
Originally published in Japan in 2001 by SHINSHOKAN CO., LTD.

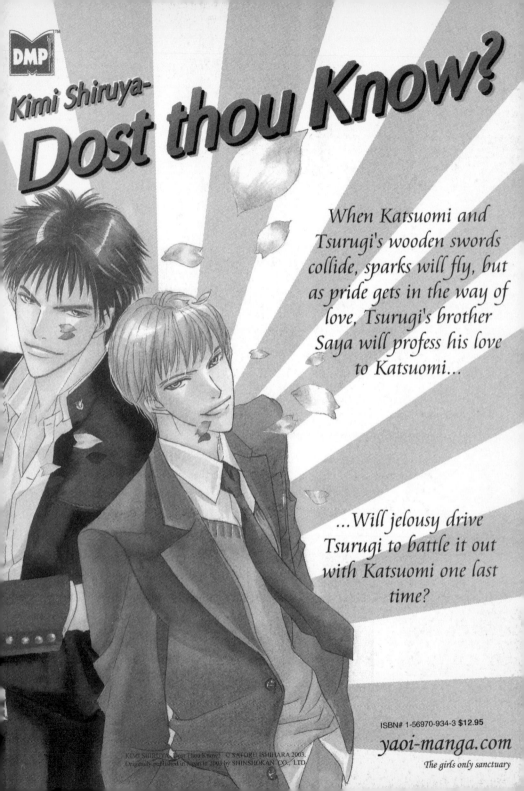

This is the back of the book! Start from the other side.

NATIVE MANGA readers read manga from *right to left*.

*If you run into our **Native Manga** logo on any of our books... you'll know that this manga is published in it's true original native Japanese right to left reading format, as it was intended. Turn to the other side of the book and start reading from right to left, top to bottom.*

*Follow the diagram to see how its done. **Surf's Up!***